Local Government Audit Law

BY REGINALD JONES

of the Middle Temple, Barrister
formerly a District Auditor and Inspector of Audit

SUPPLEMENT TO SECOND EDITION
including application to National Health Service audit

London: HMSO

Printed in the UK for the Audit Commission
at LOC Graphics Services
ISBN 011 886 067 4

London : HMSO

PREFACE

After the changes effected by the Local Government Finance Act 1982 and reflected in the second edition of this work, a period of legislative calm was eventually followed by the conferring on local government auditors by the Local Government Act 1988 (amending the 1982 Act), of extended powers to issue prohibition orders, and to apply for judicial review, in respect of apprehended illegality affecting the accounts of local authorities. Further substantial amendments to the 1982 Act followed in 1990, when the National Health Service and Community Care Act extended the functions of the Audit Commission and its appointed auditors to cover the health service, though without application to that service of the auditor's special powers relating to illegality, etc. These changes necessitated amendment of the Code of Audit Practice prepared by the Audit Commission under the 1982 Act, and a new Code was approved by Parliament and came into force in November 1990. The period since publication of the second edition has also seen an increased amount of new audit case law, including two cases reaching the House of Lords. The combined result of the abovementioned and other changes has been to produce the need for a substantial supplement, the size required increasing markedly during the course of its preparation.

The layout of the supplement follows that of the second edition. Amendments to, and comments on, any paragraph in that edition have the same number as that paragraph. Paragraphs dealing with new material receive the same number as that in the main text which they would naturally follow, but with the addition of an alphabetical suffix as appropriate. Relevant provisions of Acts and Rules of Court as amended, and the new Code of Audit Practice, are printed in full (Apps.A,B2/3,C). Entries in other appendices are limited to amendments to, and comments on, the corresponding items in the main text.

Minor amendments to the main text required by changes in the law may not have been spelt out in all cases, and readers are asked to supply such amendments for themselves where necessary, for example reading local government auditor to include health service auditor as appropriate, substituting community charges or their successors for rates, excluding references to metropolitan counties and the Greater London Council.

I must again express my gratitude to the Audit Commission and to its officers who have backed and assisted in the preparation of this supplement and reiterate that expressions of opinion are my own responsibility and have not received any official approval. Particular thanks are again due to David Smith, who has repeated the valuable help he gave in the first edition in checking references and correcting errors and omissions. And again I heartily thank my wife (the original dedication still applicable), who has once more heroically undertaken the task of translating illegible drafts into typescript.

The law is intended to be stated as at 31 August 1991.

R.J.

September 1991

CONTENTS

CONTENTS

CONTENTS

TABLE OF CASES

[References in bold type are to paragraphs where the facts of a case appear or where the fullest treatment is given of a case with numerous citations.]

TABLE OF STATUTES

[References in bold type are to paragraphs where the text of a provision is quoted or where the primary treatment is given of a provision with numerous citations.]

TABLE OF STATUTORY INSTRUMENTS AND RULES OF COURT

[References in bold type as for Table of Statutes]

TABLE OF CIRCULARS
AND CODES OF PRACTICE

(References in bold type as for Table of Statutes)

TABLE OF ABBREVIATIONS

Acts and Regulations

1933 Act, or   /1933: Local Government Act 1933.
1972 Act, or   /1972: Local Government Act 1972.
1977 Act, or   /1977: National Health Service Act 1977*
1982 Act, òr   /1982: Local Government Finance Act 1982*
1990 Act, or   /1990: National Health Service and Community Care Act 1990.*
1983 Regulations, or   /1983: Accounts and Audit Regulations 1983 (S.I. 1983/1761) (Amended provisions reproduced at App.B.1, below).

R.S.C: Rules of the Supreme Court 1965, as amended.

C.C.R: County Court Rules 1981, as amended.

* Audit provisions, as amended, reproduced at App.A, below

Circulars, etc.

[D.O.E.] Circular: Department of the Environment Circular - see Table of Circulars for Welsh Office references.
D.E.S.: Department of Education and Science
W.O.: Welsh Office.
Code of Audit Practice: Code of Audit Practice for Local Authorities and the National Health Service in England and Wales, issued November 1990, reproduced at App.C, below, - or corresponding earlier codes if the context so requires.

Books

Wade: Wade, *Administrative Law,* 6th edn., 1988.
Cross: Cross on *Evidence,* 7th edn., 1990.

Bodies

'Authority' or 'local authority', unless the context otherwise requires, includes all bodies, or all local government bodies, subject to audit under Part III of the Local Government Finance Act 1982.
'Parochial authority', unless the context otherwise requires, includes parish councils and meetings, charter trustees, community councils, and joint committees thereof.
'Principal councils': councils of counties, districts and London boroughs (together with the Common Council of the City of London and the Council of the Isles of Scilly unless the context otherwise requires).
'Health service body': bodies listed at 2.30E below, subject to audit under Part III/1982 as amended by the 1990 Act (also referred to in Code of Audit Practice as 'health authorities').
'[Audit] Commission': The Audit Commission for Local Authorities and the National Health Service in England and Wales.

Other Abbreviations

CIPFA: The Chartered Institute of Public Finance and Accountancy.
SSAP: Statement of Standard Accounting Practice (4.55, main text).
SORP: Statement of Recommended Practice (4.55, below).
NHS: National Health Service.

CHAPTER 1

HISTORICAL DEVELOPMENT

1.54A The history of local government audit law since the publication of the second edition of this book has not been without incident. A brief summary of the more important developments is given here in continuation of Chapter 1 of the main text. More detailed consideration is given as appropriate elsewhere in the supplement.

1.54B In 1985 delay of 2-3 months in setting a rate by Liverpool City Council and Lambeth London Borough Council resulted in audit action which led finally to the first decision of the House of Lords on local government audit law since 1925 and only the second in the long history of the subject. The delay arose as a result of opposition by the councillors to Government policy in reducing grants to local authorities, with consequential attempts to persuade the Government to increase their grants. The respective district auditors, after giving the councillors opportunity to make representations in writing and considering their responses, certified sums due from them in each case as losses caused by their wilful misconduct.

1.54C Each set of councillors appealed to the High Court. Both appeals were dismissed, the court holding that the delay in rate- making was for the improper reason of putting pressure on the Government by the threat of chaos and was therefore unlawful, that the councillors in disregarding advice to that effect were guilty of wilful misconduct, and that the auditors had not acted unfairly in inviting representations in writing rather than orally. The Court of Appeal dismissed a further appeal by the Liverpool councillors, who then appealed to the House of Lords, where their arguments were directed almost entirely to the question of the fairness of the auditor's procedure. On this issue their Lordships held that in all the circumstances, including the facts that the councillors had not requested an oral hearing and that they had been able to make full written representations, the auditor had not acted unfairly in not affording them an oral hearing and they had not been prejudiced by his failure to do so (*Lloyd* v. *McMahon,* [1987] A.C. 625).

1.54D The audit system was again the subject of review in 1986 by the Committee of Inquiry into the Conduct of Local Authority Business, under the chairmanship of David Widdicombe Q.C. The committee recommended that the auditors' powers under section 19 and 20 of the Local Government Finance Act 1982 should be transferred to the Audit Commission and that the procedures leading to surcharge and disqualification under section 20 in respect of loss due to wilful misconduct and failure to bring into account should be brought into line with those of section 19 relating to unlawful items of account, except that in both cases there should be a duty rather than a discretion to apply to the court. They also recommended that rights of objection should be extended to ratepayers, and that the Audit Commission should be given new powers to seek injunctions and orders of mandamus against local authorities to prevent them from incurring unlawful expenditure, or to compel them to take action required by law where failure to do so would result in financial loss. To improve publicity for auditors' reports the committee proposed that the chief executive of an authority should be placed under a statutory duty to notify all councillors immediately of the receipt of a report, to provide a copy to councillors on request, and to make copies available for public inspection.

1.54E The Government took action in 1988 in respect of one aspect of the Widdicombe recommendations, the need for powers of early intervention to challenge unlawful expenditure or unlawful loss. The new powers were conferred on the auditors rather than on the Audit Commission, however. The Local Government Act 1988 inserted new sections in the Local Government Finance Act 1982 which empowered the auditor to issue a prohibition order requiring a body or officer under audit to desist from making or implementing a decision or taking action which the auditor has reason to believe would result in unlawful items of account or would be unlawful and likely to cause a loss or deficiency (s.25A). The body (but not an officer) may appeal to the High Court against a prohibition order. Subject to any decision on appeal, any action in contravention of a prohibition order will be unlawful (s.25B). The auditor is also empowered to make application for judicial review of any decision of a body under audit, or of any failure by the body to act, which in either case it is reasonable to believe would have an effect on the accounts of the body (s.25D).

1.54F In July 1988 the Government issued a White Paper setting out its response to other matters raised by the Widdicombe Committee. It rejected the recommendation that responsibility for taking action under sections 19 and 20 of the 1982 Act should be transferred from auditors to the Audit Commission. Nor did it accept that section 20 procedures should be brought into line with those of section 19. It accepted the recommendation that the right of objection to the accounts should be extended to all ratepayers, including business ratepayers who might not be locally resident, but no action was taken on this before the abolition of domestic rates and the introduction of the uniform business rate. On publicity for the auditor's report the Government accepted the need for improvements along the lines proposed, which were eventually effected by the Local Government Finance (Publicity for Auditors' Reports) Act 1991, introduced as a private member's Bill supported by the Government.

1.54G The Education Reform Act 1988 conferred limited functions on the Audit Commission in respect of those sectors of educational provision which the Act removed from local authority control. At the request of the Polytechnics and Colleges Funding Council, a higher education corporation or the governing body of a grant-maintained school, the Commission may undertake studies in respect of their economy, efficiency and effectiveness. Also, at the request of a higher education corporation or a grant-maintained school, the Commission may advise them on their audit appointments and arrange for the accounts to be audited by officers of the Commission if the bodies so desire.

1.54H The Local Government and Housing Act 1989 (s.11) varied the effect of the provisions of section 17 of the Local Government Finance Act 1982 to secure that the public rights of inspection of accounts and questioning the auditor should not extend to personal information about an individual member of staff held in respect of his employment. This reversed the effect of the case of *Oliver v. Northampton B.C.* (1987), 151 J.P. 44, in which it was held that rights under section 17 of the 1982 Act extended to details of both gross and net payments to employees, so that details of deductions for tax etc., even attachment of earnings orders where applicable, could be disclosed.

1.54I The phenomenon of 'creative accounting', by which a variety of ingenious schemes were used by some local authorities to avoid or mitigate the effect of central government controls on spending, led to a number of cases in the late 1980s in which the courts upheld audit action to question the legality of some of the schemes. In *R. v. District Auditor No. 3 District, ex parte West Yorkshire Metropolitan County Council* (1985), 26 R.V.R. 24, the court declared invalid the creation of a trust to carry forward to a subsequent year the unexpended balance of the 'free twopenny rate' which was allowed for expenditure in the interests of the area or its inhabitants under section 137 of the Local Government Act 1972. In *Leicester City Council v. District Auditor for Leicester* (1985), 29 R.V.R. 162, the court upheld the auditor's view that pay of officers engaged on functions authorised under section 137 should be charged to the account of expenditure under that section. In *Stockdale* v. *Haringey L.B.C.*, [1989] R.A. 107, the court upheld an application for judicial review by the auditor, rejecting the council's contention that the re-advance to spending accounts of money previously repaid to the loans fund was not caught by the statutory limit on borrowing powers. In *R.* v. *Wirral M.B.C, ex parte Milstead* (1989), 87 L.G.R. 611, the court granted the auditor's application for judicial review to quash as unlawful the council's decision to enter into a factoring agreement under which they would sell, for a current payment, the right to anticipated receipts from future sales of land (the object being to increase current capital receipts and hence the statutory limit of capital expenditure for the year).

1.54J An audit case to hit the headlines of the city pages was *Hazell* v. *Hammersmith and Fulham L.B.C.*, [1991] 2 W.L.R. 372. The case concerned 'interest rate swaps' and the like, by which for example, a borrower at fixed interest contracts with a third party to pay or receive the difference between his interest liability on that basis and what it would have been at variable interest - or *vice versa* for a borrower at variable interest. A considerable number of local authorities had entered into such arrangements for the purpose of interest rate risk management, but the extent of the Hammersmith Council's use of the devices was such as to indicate that they were used for trading purposes with the object of making a profit. The auditor applied under section 19 of the Local Government Finance Act 1982 for a declaration that the items of account reflecting the transactions were contrary to law. The council, having taken their own legal advice, did not dispute the application, but a number of banks involved in the transactions were joined as respondents. The Divisional Court allowed the application, holding that it was beyond the powers of local authorities to enter into interest rate swaps or any other methods of interest rate risk management which are not expressly referred to in legislation. The banks appealed and the Court of Appeal allowed the appeal in part, holding that swap transactions entered into as interest rate risk management with reference to a particular debt were within an authority's powers as incidental to the power of borrowing. They held, however, that local authorities were not empowered to carry on a trade of entering into swaps and the like with a view to profit and that the majority of the council's transactions were unlawful because tainted with the improper purpose of trading. The House of Lords, on appeal by the auditor, reinstated the Divisional Court decision that all interest rate swaps and similar transactions were outside the powers of local authorities, since the very detailed provisions of the Local Government Act 1972 provided a code which defined and limited borrowing powers and prevented activities such as swaps being treated as incidental to the borrowing function.

1.54K The National Health Service and Community Care Act 1990 extended the responsibilities of the Commission and its appointed auditors to bodies administering the National Health Service. The Commission's title became 'The Audit Commission for Local Authorities and the National Health Service in England and Wales'. It became responsible for appointing the auditors of health service bodies, including regional and district health authorities, family health service authorities, NHS trusts established under the 1990 Act, and fund-holding medical practices in respect of sums allotted to them under that Act. The Commission also became responsible for the same functions in respect of those bodies as it held in respect of local government bodies (para.1.52, main text) with the exception of the function, under section 27 of the 1982 Act, of undertaking studies as to the impact of statutory provisions and ministerial directions and guidance on economy, efficiency and effectiveness in services.

1.54L The 1990 Act did not confer on the auditors of health service bodies the powers and duties of local government auditors under sections 19, 20 and 25A-25D of the 1982 Act relating to illegality, failure to account, loss caused by wilful misconduct, prohibition orders, and application for judicial review. Nor did it apply to health service bodies the rights of local government electors, under sections 17 and 24 of the 1982 Act, to inspect accounts and audit reports and to challenge accounts. It did apply the 1982 Act powers and duties of auditors, with minor modifications, under sections 15 (general duties of auditors) 16 (auditor's right to obtain documents and information) and 18 (auditor's reports) (s.20, Sch.4). In relation to illegality, section 20(3) of the 1990 Act required the auditor of a health service body to refer to the Secretary of State any cases where he has reason to believe that the body has acted or is about to act unlawfully in incurring expenditure or in action likely to cause loss or deficiency.

1.54M The new responsibilities of the Audit Commission naturally involved a large increase in the work of its appointed auditors. The District Audit Service absorbed most of the audit staff of the Department of Health and Welsh Office formerly employed on health audit and a reorganisation of the service followed. The title of Chief Inspector of Audit disappeared after some 70 years (120 if Inspector of Audits is included), but responsibility under the Controller for the service remained under the new title of Director of Audit, assisted by seven regional directors. For the Commission's officers appointed as statutory auditors of local authorities and health service bodies, the title of District Auditor again happily survives.

CHAPTER 2

LOCAL GOVERNMENT AND HEALTH SERVICE AUDITS AND AUDITORS

I AUDIT UNDER LOCAL GOVERNMENT FINANCE ACT 1982

2.2A   The National Health Service and Community Care Act 1990 extended the Audit Commission's responsibilities under the 1982 Act to health service bodies (2.30E, below), and its full title became 'The Audit Commission for Local Authorities and the National Health Service in England and Wales' (s.11(1)/1982, as amended by s.20 and Sch.4/1990). The auditors appointed by the Commission became responsible under the 1982 Act for auditing the accounts of the health service bodies, albeit with modified audit provisions.

II BODIES SUBJECT TO AUDIT

General

2.3   Audit under Part III of the Local Government Finance Act 1982 has also been applied to:

Joint authorities established by or under the Local Government Act 1985 (2.30A, below)

The Inner London Education Authority, until its abolition (2.30B)

Residuary bodies established by the Local Government Act 1985 and the London Pensions Fund Authority, but with modified audit provisions (2.30C)

The Broads Authority (2.30D)

Health service bodies, but with modified audit provisions (2.30E-I)

The provisions relating to the City of London and probation committees have been amended (2.5, 2.26)

The Greater London Council and the London Transport Executive were abolished by the Local Government Act 1985 and the London Regional Transport Act 1984 respectively.

The Water Act 1989 (s.136, Sch.15) transferred responsibility for main river drainage from water authorities to the National Rivers Authority, whose auditor is appointed by the Secretary of State (Sch.1, para.22). Where the Authority acts as an internal drainage board under section 4, Land Drainage Act 1991, the audit of its accounts as drainage board remains subject to Part III of the Local Government Finance Act 1982 under section 12(2)(j) thereof; the Audit Commission may appoint the same auditor as the Secretary of State.

The City of London

2.5   For financial years 1990/1 onwards section 12(3)(a) of the 1982 Act, referring to the rate fund accounts of the City of London, is amended to read: 'the accounts of the collection fund of the Common Council and the accounts of the City fund' (Local Government Finance Act 1988, s.137, Sch.12, paras.3(2),(5)). The City fund, established by section 93 of the Local Government Finance Act 1988, is equivalent to the general fund that other charging authorities are required to maintain under section 91 of that Act.

The reference in section 12(3)(b) of the 1982 Act to 1974 and 1977 Regulations is now to be construed as a reference to the Local Government Superannuation Regulations 1986 (S.I. 1986/24), by which the former regulations were revoked (Interpretation Act 1978, ss.17(2)(a), 23(1)).

2.6   In lines 5 and 6, for 'rates or rate fund services' read 'community charges (or their successors) or general/county fund services'.

Parish meetings

2.10   In line 7, for 's.150(4)', read 'Local Government Finance Act 1988, ss.68, 144(2)'.

2.11   As regards the references to 'rating authority' in lines 4 and 14 of page 24, and to 'relief of general rates' in line 5, it appears that the substitution of 'charging authority' and 'relief of community charges (or their successors)' would generally meet the intention of the conditions referred to.

Police authorities

2.14   Sections 2 and 8(3) of the Police Act 1964 were amended by the Local Government Act 1985 so that they refer only to non-metropolitan counties (s.37, Sch.11, para.1). Metropolitan county police authorities and the Northumbria Police Authority, established by Part IV of the Local Government Act 1985, being joint authorities as defined by section 105 of that Act, are audited under the Local Government Finance Act 1982 by virtue of section 12(2)(aa) thereof, inserted by section 72 of the 1985 Act.

2.15   In line 3, for 'rate fund of the City' read 'City fund'.

Passenger transport

2.18   On the abolition of metropolitan county councils by the Local Government Act 1985, a metropolitan county passenger transport authority was established for each county by Part IV of the Act. These authorities are subject to audit under the 1982 Act under section 12(2)(aa) thereof as for metropolitan county police authorities (2.14, above).

2.19   In the penultimate line, after 'press' read 'and public' (s.18(5) as amended - 4.103, below).

The provisions of section 18A in respect of publicity for immediate reports (4.110A, below) apply both to the authority and the executive (s.31(1)(ca)).

Subsidiary companies

2.20   The Companies Act definition of 'subsidiary' now appears in section 736 of the Companies Act 1985.

2.21   Section 31(4) of the Local Government Finance Act 1982 was substituted and section 31(6) amended by the Transport Act 1985, Schedule 7. Section 31(5) was amended by the Companies Consolidation (Consequential Provisions) Act 1985, Sch.2. The effect is that no question now arises of regulations being made to apply Part III of the Local Government Finance Act 1982 to subsidiaries of passenger transport executives, but that auditors of such subsidiaries must be approved by the Audit Commission.

2.23   In line 14, for 'para.21(b)' read 'para.43(b)/1990'.

2.24   In line 3, for 's.14, Companies Act 1967' read 's.235, Companies Act 1985, as substituted by s.9, Companies Act 1989'.

Probation committees

2.26   Section 12(2)(1) of the 1982 Act was amended by the Criminal Justice Act 1988, section 132 and Schedule 11, paragraph 8, to exclude the probation committee for the inner London area. This was because expenses of this committee are met by the Receiver of the Metropolitan Police, whose accounts are not audited under the 1982 Act.

Governors of educational institutions

2.28A The Education (Further and Higher Education Institutions Access Funds) Regulations 1990(S.I. 1990/1555)empower the Secretary of State to pay grant to the governing bodies of such institutions in respect of expenditure incurred in providing financial assistance to students (reg.3). Current terms and conditions for the payment of such access funds to local authority maintained or assisted further education institutions, accompanying D.E.S. Circular dated 13 March 1991 (W.O. 22 April 1991), provide that governing bodies may appoint as auditors persons eligible to audit a company, or who are CIPFA qualified, or who are appointed by the Audit Commission to audit the local authority accounts relating to the institution (para.8). The terms and conditions also provide that the auditor's report to the governing body, in addition to giving an opinion on the access fund's accounts, should say whether, in the auditor's opinion, the fund has been properly applied in accordance with the terms and conditions, and whether the system of financial management and internal controls is adequate. A copy of the report is to accompany accounts forwarded to the Department (para.9).

The appointment of auditors by governors under these terms and conditions is for the purpose of meeting requirements of the Department of Education and Science. For general audit purposes it may be considered that access funds received and disbursed by governors of an institution maintained by a local authority must be accounted for within the context of the authority's accounts and are therefore subject also to audit under Part III of the Local Government Finance Act 1982 by the auditor appointed by the Audit Commission.

Local Government Act 1985: joint authorities, residuary bodies, pensions fund authorities

2.30A Section 72 of the Local Government Act 1985, inserting paragraph (aa) in section 12(2) of the Local Government Finance Act 1982, applied audit under the 1982 Act to joint authorities established by the 1985 Act, that is, metropolitan county police authorities, the Northumbria Police Authority, metropolitan county fire and civil defence authorities, the London Fire and Civil Defence Authority and metropolitan county passenger transport authorities (ss.105, 24-28); section 12(2)(aa) also applies to authorities established by the Waste Regulation and Disposal (Authorities) Order 1985 (S.I.

1985/1884) made under section 10 of the 1985 Act (art.9(2)), and to the South Yorkshire Pensions Authority (S.I. 1987/2110, Sch.1, para.6).

2.30B Section 72 of the 1985 Act also inserted paragraph (ab) in section 12(2) of the 1982 Act, applying 1982 Act audit to the Inner London Education Authority established by that Act. (The accounts of the pre-1985 ILEA had been audited as part of the accounts of the Greater London Council, of which it was a committee). Paragraph (ab) was repealed by the Local Government and Housing Act 1989, which abolished the ILEA with effect from 1 April 1990.

2.30C For the residuary bodies set up by the 1985 Act to wind up the affairs of the abolished metropolitan county councils and the Greater London Council, section 79 of that Act applied the audit provisions of the 1982 Act with the exception of those relating to public inspection of accounts and right of challenge (s.17), illegality, failure to account and misconduct (ss.19, 20), extraordinary audit (s.22), accounts regulations (ss.15(1)(a), 23), and right to inspect statements of accounts and auditor's reports (s.24). Section 79(3),(4) of the 1985 Act confers on local government electors equivalent rights of inspection of accounts and of questioning the auditor, and also a right to draw the auditor's attention to matters on which he could make a report under section 15(3) of the 1982 Act. But no right to make objections is conferred. Copies of statements of accounts and auditors' reports are to be sent to the Secretary of State to be laid before Parliament, and any person may inspect such copies (s.79(5),(6)). The London Government Reorganisation (Pensions etc.) Order 1989, S.I. 1989/1815, applied section 79 of the 1985 Act to the London Pensions Fund Authority set up by the Order, with an additional provision empowering the Secretary of State to direct an extraordinary audit under section 22(2) of the 1982 Act.

The Broads Authority

2.30D Section 17 of the Norfolk and Suffolk Broads Act 1988, inserting paragraph (ff) in section 12(2) of the Local Government Finance Act 1982, made the new Broads Authority established by the 1988 Act subject to audit under the 1982 Act. Section 17 of the 1988 Act also inserted a new section 36(3) in the 1982 Act, specifying that references to local government electors should cover electors for all participating authorities under the 1988 Act, and that the Broads Authority and the Navigation Committee under the 1988 Act should each be taken to be a local authority for the purposes of sections 19 and 20 of the 1982 Act (see ss.19(2)(b) and 20(4) relating to disqualification).

Health service bodies

2.30E The National Health Service and Community Care Act 1990 made the following bodies subject to audit under Part III of the Local Government Finance Act 1982, but with modified audit provisions:

Regional health authorities

District health authorities

Special health authorities established by the Secretary of State under section 11 of the National Health Service Act 1977

Special trustees for university or teaching hospitals appointed by the Secretary of State under section 29 of the National Health Service Reorganisation Act 1973 and section 95(1) of the 1977 Act

Family health services authorities (formerly family practitioner committees)

The Dental Practice Board

NHS trusts established under section 5 of the 1990 Act

Members of fund-holding practices recognised under section 14 of the 1990 Act in relation to allotted sums paid to them under section 15 of that Act.

These bodies are comprised in the term 'health service bodies', as defined in section 12(5) of the 1982 Act, inserted by Schedule 4 of the 1990 Act (para.2(3)), and also in the term 'health authorities' as used in the Code of Audit Practice (para.7).

2.30F Except for the bodies first established by the 1990 Act (NHS trusts and fund-holding practices) the bodies listed above were formerly audited under section 98(1) of the 1977 Act by auditors appointed by the Secretary of State for Health. Section 184(1) of the Local Government and Housing Act 1989 inserted a new section 28A in the 1982 Act, a transitional provision which empowered the Audit Commission, at the request of the Secretary of State, to appoint auditors of the bodies specified in section 98(1), to undertake studies designed to improve economy, efficiency and effectiveness of those bodies, and to advise on the transfer to the Commission of responsibility for the audit of the bodies. This provision was repealed by the 1990 Act on the coming into force of section 20 of that Act, which amended section 98(1) of the 1977 Act to provide that the bodies to which that section applied should be audited by auditors appointed by the Audit Commission. Schedule 4 of the 1990 Act amended Part III of the Local Government Act 1982 to apply it to these audits (para.2(1), inserting s.12(2)(ea)/1982), subject to exclusions and modifications detailed under the relevant chapters and headings below. The main exclusions are those relating to the rights of local government electors (ss.17, 24), to the power to make regulations (s.23) and to illegality, failure to account and misconduct (ss.19, 20, 25A-D); lesser duties of auditors of health service bodies in respect of illegality are enacted by section 20(3) of the 1990 Act (5.6B, below).

2.30G Paragraph 24 of Schedule 2 to the 1990 Act, inserting paragraph (bbb) into section 98(1) of the 1977 Act, made NHS Trusts subject to audit under that section and hence to the provisions of Part III of the 1982 Act as amended for health service bodies. As to members of fund-holding practices, section 12(3A)-(3C) of the 1982 Act (inserted by Sch.4/1990) provides that accounts relating to allotted sums shall be subject to audit under the 1982 Act, but that regulations may provide that in specified circumstances and to a specified extent, the audit provisions of the 1982 Act shall not apply to those accounts if they are submitted to a family health service authority and summarised in that authority's accounts (as they are required to be by s.98(2B)/1977, as inserted by s.20(2)/1990). The Code of Audit Practice indicates that in that case the auditor should seek to rely on analytical review techniques with any detailed audit procedures carried out on a cyclical basis (para.85).

2.30H Section 98(1) of the 1977 Act provides that the Comptroller and Auditor General may examine all accounts subject to audit under that subsection and any records relating to them and any report of the auditor on them. Section 98(2B), as inserted by s.20(2)/1990, makes similar provisions in respect of fund-holding practices. Section 98(4) requires the Secretary of State to submit summarised accounts of the health authorities and special trustees and a statement of accounts of the Dental Practice Board to the Comptroller and Auditor General who shall examine and certify them and lay copies with his report on them before both Houses of Parliament. Section 6 of the National Audit Act 1983 empowers the Comptroller and Auditor General to carry out examinations into the economy, efficiency and effectiveness (but not to question the merits of policy objectives) of bodies required to keep accounts under section 98, that is, those listed at 2.30E above.

2.30I The audit provisions of the 1990 Act came into force on 1 October 1990, apart from some minor exceptions with an appointed day of 5 July 1990 (National Health

Service and Community Care Act 1990 (Commencement No.1) Order 1990 (S.I. 1990/1329)). Section 33(4A) of the 1982 Act (inserted by Sch.4/1990) empowered the Secretary of State to provide by regulation for former provisions for health service audits to continue to apply with modification to accounts for periods before that date. The National Health Service (Audit of Accounts) (Transitional Provisions) Regulations 1990 (S.I. 1990/1842) provided for the former provisions to apply to accounts for the year ended 31 March 1990.

III   AUDIT OF PARTICULAR CLASSES OF ACCOUNTS

Accounts of officers

2.31   Section 25 of the 1982 Act is amended by Schedule 4 to the National Health Service and Community Care Act 1990 to provide that an officer of a health service body is subject only to the same provisions of Part III of the 1982 Act as is the body itself.

In note 9, for reference to 1974 Regulations read '1986 (S.I. 1986/24, reg.B1(3))'.

Charity and trust accounts

Trusts of health service bodies

2.42A Section 90 of the National Health Service Act 1977, following similar earlier provisions, provides that a health authority has power to accept, hold and administer any property on trust for all or any purposes relating to the health services. For a number of university and teaching hospitals special trustees were appointed by the Secretary of State under section 29 of the National Health Service Reorganisation Act 1973 (repeated in section 95 of the 1977 Act) to hold and administer trust property relating to the hospital(s) for which they were appointed. Under section 98(1)(d) of the 1977 Act as amended, the accounts of special trustees are subject to audit by auditors appointed by the Audit Commission and to examination by the Comptroller and Auditor General. Trust accounts of other health service bodies subject to such audit and examination under section 98(1) of the 1977 Act are so audited and examined as accounts to be kept by the body under that section.

2.42B Because special trustees had no corporate status and this created some administrative difficulties in the day-to-day running of funds, a few special trustees set up holding companies under their sole control for the purpose of holding their trust property. Following questions raised by the Comptroller and Auditor General as to the legality of these arrangements, the Department of Health instructed special trustees, in a letter of 12 December 1977, that their accounts and supporting records submitted to audit must be as complete and detailed, in respect of transactions of such created companies, as if the services of the companies were not involved.

IV   THE AUDIT COMMISSION

Constitution

2.52   The National Health Service and Community Care Act 1990 extended the Commission's responsibilities to health service bodies (2.30E, above) and its full title became 'The Audit Commission for Local Authorities and the National Health Service in England and Wales' (s.11(1)/1982, as amended by Sch.4/1990). Section 11(2) was amended by the 1990 Act (Sch.4) to provide that the Commission shall consist of 15 to 20 members appointed by the Secretary of State after consultation with such organisations and other bodies as appear to him to be appropriate.

2.53   Paragraph 9 of Schedule 3 to the 1982 Act was amended by Schedule 4 to the 1990 Act to provide that the requirement to manage the Commission's affairs so that income covers expenditure applies separately to its functions in relation to health service bodies.

Officers

2.54   Section 20(4)-(7) of the 1990 Act made provision, similar to that under paragraph 8 of Schedule 3 to the 1982 Act, for the Commission to offer employment on no-worsening terms to civil servants formerly employed on the audit of health service bodies.

2.55   Reorganisation of the staff of the Audit Commission has resulted in the elimination of the post of Deputy Controller and the grade of deputy district auditor, a change of title of the Chief Inspector of Audit to Director of Audit, the inclusion in the structure of seven regional directors, and the renaming of assistant district auditors as managers.

Functions

2.56   For 'Government grants and contracts' read 'Certification of grant claims etc'. The following headings are to be added:

Passenger transport (2.21, above)

National Health Service (2.30F, above)

2.57   Section 29(3) of the 1982 Act was amended by Schedule 4 to the 1990 Act to extend it to the audit by agreement of bodies which appear to the Secretary of State to be connected with the National Health Service.

2.58A The Education Reform Act 1988 removed from the local government field grant-maintained schools and higher education institutions falling under the provisions of sections 52 and 121-2 of that Act, and their accounts therefore ceased to be subject to audit under the Local Government Finance Act 1982. However, the Commission may, on request, undertake or promote studies designed to improve economy, efficiency and effectiveness in the management or operations of the Polytechnics and Colleges Funding Council, a higher education corporation or the governing body of a grant- maintained school. The request may be made by the body itself; additionally, the Funding Council may ask for studies relating to a higher education corporation (Education Reform Act 1988, s.220(1), (2)).

2.58B The Commission may, at the request of a higher education corporation or the governing body of a grant-maintained school, advise them on the appointment of auditors and arrange for audit by officers of the Commission (*ibid.*, s.220(4),(5)). Higher education corporations are required to consult the Commission before appointing auditors for their first financial year. Their auditors must be members of specified accountancy bodies, including the Chartered Institute of Public Finance and Accountancy (*ibid.*, Sch.7, para.18(4),(5)). The Funding Council may seek the Commission's advice in directing higher education corporations in the preparation of statements of accounts, which are to be subject to audit (s.220(3),(5); Sch.7, para.18(1)-(3)). Services provided by the Commission under this and the foregoing paragraphs are to be charged at full cost (s.220(6)).

2.58C Section 70(5) of the Local Government and Housing Act 1989 provides that an order made by the Secretary of State under section 70(1) in respect of requirements for companies under the control or influence of local authorities (*post,* para.6.40F) may require a company or local authority to obtain the consent of the Audit Commission before taking any particular action or course of action.

Audit fees

2.59   The reference to consultation in line 2 now extends to health service organisations (s.21(2A)/1982, inserted by Sch.4/1990).

Functions of the Secretary of State

2.60   Sub-paragraph (10) should be replaced by 'Approving the auditors of subsidiaries of passenger transport executives (s.31(4)/1982 as substituted by Sch.7, Transport Act 1985)'.

2.60A The Secretary of State has the following functions in respect of the accounts and audit of health service bodies:

(1)   Directing, with the approval of the Treasury, the form in which accounts of health service bodies shall be kept (National Health Service Act 1977, s.98(1), s.98(2B)(a), as inserted by National Health Service and Community Care Act 1990, s.20(2));

(2)   Directing, with the approval of the Treasury, the form in which annual accounts of health service bodies other than fund- holding practices shall be prepared and submitted to the Secretary of State, and in the case of NHS trusts, the methods and principles according to which the accounts are to be prepared and the information to be given in the accounts (s.98(2)/1977; s.98(2B)/1977, as inserted by para.24, Sch.2/1990);

(3)   Preparing, in such form as the Treasury may direct, summarised accounts of health service bodies, other than fund- holding practices and the Dental Practice Board, and a statement of accounts of that Board, and transmitting them to the Comptroller and Auditor General (s.98(4)/1977);

(4)   Directing, with the approval of the Treasury, the form in which fund-holding practices shall prepare accounts in respect of allotted sums and submit them to the family health services authorities, and the form in which those authorities shall include in their accounts summarised versions of fund-holding practices' accounts (s.98(2B)/1977, as inserted by s.20(2)/1990);

(5)   Receiving references from auditors of health service bodies under section 20(3) of the National Health Service and Community Care Act 1990 in respect of believed unlawful expenditure or unlawful action likely to cause loss or deficiency;

(6)   Regulating the timing of the offer of no-worsening terms to health service audit staff and naming the staff concerned (s.20(4)/1990);

(7)   Making regulations defining circumstances and extent in and to which accounts of fund-holding practices may not be subject to audit under the Local Government Finance Act 1982 (s.12(3B)/1982);

(8)   Approval on the recommendation of the Commission of auditors not otherwise qualified (s.13(5),(5A)/1982);

(9)   Receiving copies of auditors' reports on health service bodies (s.18(4)/1982 as amended);

(10) Providing by regulations for continuance of statutory provision relating to audit of accounts for periods before the appointed day for application of audit under the 1982 Act (s.33(4A)/1982);

(11) Giving directions to health authorities and family health service authorities in respect of their financial duties under sections 97A and 97B of the 1977 Act (ss.97A(4)-(7), 97B(2)-(4)/1977);

(12) Making regulations and giving directions in respect of the regulation of financial arrangements of health authorities, family health service authorities and the Dental Practice Board (s.99/1977).

2.61   Directions under paragraph 3 of Schedule 3 to the 1982 Act, as amended by the 1990 Act, must be preceded, if the case so requires, by consultation with such organisations connected with the health service as appear to the Secretary of State to be appropriate.

2.62   The functions in respect of health service bodies listed in paragraph 2.60A above will presumably be carried out in England by the Secretary of State for Health.

V AUDITORS

Appointment

2.63   The requirement for consultation with the body concerned before appointment of an auditor does not apply to health service bodies (s.13(3)/1982, as amended by Sch.4/1990).

Qualifications

2.66   Section 13(5) of the 1982 Act, as amended by Schedule 4 to the 1990 Act, now provides that a person for the time being approved by the Secretary of State on the recommendation of the Commission (though not otherwise qualified under section 13) may be appointed by the Commission as an auditor of accounts under Part III of the 1982 Act. Section 13(5A) limits this power of approval to the period ending 31 March 1996, but persons approved at that date will continue to be approved for the purpose of the section unless the approval is withdrawn.

Officers of the Commission: District Auditors

2.69   From October 1990 England and Wales is divided for the purpose of allocation of audits into seven regions, the regional directors' offices being in Leeds (No.1), Chorley (No.2), Birmingham (No.3), Cardiff (No.4), Stevenage (No.5), Winchester (No.6) and London (No.7).

Auditors other than officers of the Commission

2.70,n.16   Section 161(4) of the Companies Act 1948 was re-enacted on consolidation as section 389(8) of the Companies Act 1985. This provision has been repealed by the Companies Act 1989, which enacts new provisions as to eligibility to conduct company audits, including a general provision allowing the appointment of firms, defined as bodies corporate or partnerships (ss.25(2), 53(1)).

Audit staff

2.71   A question may arise whether the requirement that the auditor must exercise personally his powers under sections 19 and 20 of the 1982 Act (now in para.70 of the 1990 Code of Audit Practice) means that he must also undertake personally the hearing of objections under section 17(3)(a) as to any matter on which action could be taken under section 19 or 20. In *R. v. Director of Public Prosecutions, ex parte Association of First Division Civil Servants* (1988), 138 N.L.J. 158, the Divisional Court, on application for judicial review, declared that the D.P.P. could not lawfully delegate to any person other than a crown prosecutor an initial role in the course of proceedings, involving a decision whether, in certain classes of case, the evidence was sufficient to proceed and the prosecution was in the public interest. However, that case turned on a statutory duty of the D.P.P. to take over the conduct of criminal proceedings (crown prosecutors having the powers of the D.P.P. in that respect). The court held that 'conduct' included the taking of any steps in relation to the proceedings. It thus appears that the case is distinguishable from that of the auditor who is required to exercise personally his powers under sections 19 and 20. It is clear that he cannot delegate a positive decision to apply to the court under section 19 or certify a sum due under section 20, but it does not follow that decisions not to apply or not to certify must be taken personally. Objections apart, decisions that no action is required under sections 19 and 20 are in effect an automatic result of satisfactory checks by audit staff. Moreover, it is not inconsistent with decisions being taken personally by the auditor for the hearing of an objection to be delegated. The arrangement could be for the person holding the hearing to report thereon to the auditor, who would then decide on the matter. This procedure would be similar to arrangements for public inquiries where an inspector is appointed to hold the inquiry but reports back to the relevant minister in whose name the decision is taken. It does not therefore appear that the delegation of the hearing of objections is precluded as a matter of construction of the Code of Practice. It is necessary, however, that any such delegation should be in accordance with arrangements approved by the Commission under section 13(8) of the 1982 Act.

2.72   As to deputy and assistant district auditors, see 2.55, above.

Independence of the auditor

2.79   In line 3, for 'his' read 'all'. In line 5, for 'para.4', read 'para.5/1990'.

2.80   On page 45, for 'para.7', read 'para.10/1990'; for 'para.8', read 'para.11/1990'; for '£5000', read '£10,000 (to be revised annually by the Commission)'.

VI   EXTRAORDINARY AUDITS

Direction of an extraordinary audit

2.81   As amended by Schedule 4 to the 1990 Act, section 22(1) of the 1982 Act does not provide for an extraordinary audit of a health service body to be directed on the application of a local government elector.

2.85   In last line, for 'para.12', read 'para.69/1990'.

2.89,n.21   For 'p.377' of *Wade* read '(6th edn.), p.422'.

Application of audit provisions to extraordinary audits

2.91   As amended by Schedule 4 to the 1990 Act, section 22(3) of the 1982 Act applies
to the extraordinary audit of a health service body only sections 13, 15, 16 and 18 of the
1982 Act, powers under sections 17, 19 and 20 being excluded as for an ordinary audit
of a health service body.

2.93   The form of opinion and certificate for an ordinary audit included in the
Appendix to the 1990 Code of Audit Practice (App.C, below) carries the same implication
as that referred to in the last three lines of the original paragraph.

CHAPTER 3

ACCOUNTS

I ACCOUNTS OF LOCAL AUTHORITIES – GENERAL STATUTORY PROVISIONS

Principal councils' funds and accounts

3.2   The references to the Greater London Council in section 148(2),(4) of the Local Government Act 1972 were repealed by the Local Government Act 1985. Further provisions in respect of principal councils' fund and accounts, largely replacing those of sections 147 and 148 of the 1972 Act, were made by the Local Government Finance Act 1987, the Local Government Finance Act 1988 and the Local Government and Housing Act 1989 (3.2A-C, below). The Local Government Finance (Repeals and Consequential Amendments) Order 1991, S.I. 1991/1730, repealed sections 147 and 148(1),(3) of the 1972 Act, and amended section 148(4),(5) to fit the changes noted at 3.2B.

3.2A   The Local Government Finance Act 1987, sections 1 and 2, required local authorities to maintain revenue accounts in respect of their general rate funds, county funds, or in the case of joint authorities, general funds, and defined income and expenditure to be included in and excluded from those accounts. These provisions were made in the context of the rate support grant system then in operation, which the Local Government Finance Act 1988 replaced by a new revenue support grant system from 1 April, 1990. Further provision in respect of charges to revenue accounts was made by sections 41 and 42 of the Local Government and Housing Act 1989 (3.2C, below). Sections 1 and 2 of the 1987 Act were not repealed or amended either by the 1988 Act or the 1989 Act. But the sections refer to a general rate fund revenue account in the case of district councils and London borough councils, and section 91(6) of the 1988 Act removes, from 1 April, 1990, the requirement for these authorities to keep a general rate fund and transfers the balance thereof to general fund. It may therefore be doubted whether the above provisions of the 1987 Act now have any application to these authorities.

3.2B   The Local Government Finance Act 1988 required district councils and London borough councils, as charging authorities for the community charge, to maintain from 1 April, 1990, a collection fund and, in place of a general rate fund, a general fund to which rate fund balances were to be transferred (ss.89, 91). Similar provisions apply to the City of London (ss.93, 94). Collection funds are credited with the proceeds of the community charge and, in England, with revenue support grant and shares of the non-domestic rate pool, and debited with precepts and transfers to general funds of amounts calculated as required to meet general fund net expenditure and provide necessary reserves (ss.90, 95, 97). (In Wales, revenue support grant and shares of non-domestic rates are paid direct to counties and such receipts are not therefore credited to collection accounts: s.90(3)).

3.2C   Under section 41 of the Local Government and Housing Act 1989 all expenditure of a local authority except that excluded under section 42 (3.2D, below) must be charged to a revenue account, either an account which the authority is required to keep by statute or to comply with proper practices, or which it decides to keep in accordance with proper practices. As to the meaning of 'proper practices' see 4.50A, below. Expenditure is normally to be charged in the year in which it is incurred, that is, when the authority becomes liable to make payment for it, unless it is appropriate in accordance with proper practices to charge it to an earlier or later year, (ss.41(1), 66(2)(a)). Expenditure for this purpose also includes, under section 41(3):

(a) amounts set aside, other than from capital receipts, as provisions to meet credit liabilities (3.16, below); and

(b) amounts set aside as provisions for contingencies (any liability or loss which is likely or certain to be incurred but is uncertain as to the amount or the date on which it will arise or both).

3.2D   Expenditure excluded by section 42(2) of the 1989 Act from the requirement to charge to revenue account (but which may be so charged if consistent with proper practices) is mainly expenditure for capital purposes (defined by section 40) which is capitalised by virtue of a ministerial credit approval (para.(c) of s.42(2)) or met out of capital receipts (paras.(e), (f)) or met out of money provided by another person, excluding grants from a European Community institution (para.(g)). Also so excluded by section 42(2) are superannuation and trust fund transactions (paras.(h), (i)), the repayment of the principal of borrowed money and discharge of liabilities under credit arrangements (paras.(a), (b)) and the making of investments approved by regulations under the Act - currently the Local Authorities (Capital Finance) (Approved Investments) Regulations 1990, S.I. 1990/426 (para.(d)).

II   STATUTORY PROVISIONS RELATING TO PARTICULAR AC-COUNTS OF LOCAL AUTHORITIES

Separate accounts required by law

3.5   The following amendments are required to the table of separate accounts required by law:

Service	Statutory provisions
Additions	
Airports - provision of services for associated companies	S.24, Airports Act 1986
Collection fund	S.89, Local Government Finance Act 1988
Direct service organisations -defined activities subject to competitive tendering	S.9, Local Government Act 1988
Further education establishments - supply of goods and services	S.3(4), Further Education Act 1985
Loans for economic development at less than market rates	Reg.9, Local Government (Promotion of Economic Development) Regulations 1990 (S.I. 1990/763)

Service	*Statutory provisions*
Publicity	S.5, Local Government Act 1986
Trading undertakings	S.1 and para.3, Sch.1, Local Government Finance Act 1987
Metropolitan debt administration funds - orders under Local Government Act 1985, s.66	S.1 and para.13, Sch.1, Local Government Finance Act 1987

Deletions

Loans funds }	(Paras.15 and 16, Sch.13, Local Government Act 1972 repealed by Local Government and Housing Act 1989, Sch.12)
Special funds }	

Variation of statutory provision

Advances for acquisition of houses (under Small Dwellings Acquisition Act 1899-1923)	Para.8(4), Sch.18, Housing Act 1985
Housing Revenue Account }	Ss.74, 77, Local Government and Housing Act 1989
Housing Repairs Account }	
Superannuation funds	Reg.P1, Local Government Superannuation Regulations 1986 (S.I. 1986/24)

3.6   For 's.43, Housing (Financial Provisions) Act 1958' read 's.435, Housing Act 1985 and its predecessors'.

The entries under the heading 'Rates' are no longer applicable: Local Government Finance Act 1988, Part IX.

As to trading undertakings, see now the entry under 3.5, above.

Section 41(2) of the Local Government and Housing Act 1989 defines 'revenue account' to include revenue accounts which the authority are required or decide to keep in accordance with proper practices. This indicates that separate revenue accounts may be kept within the general fund or county fund, and would apparently enable separate revenue accounts to be kept for such reserves as the authority decide to maintain in accordance with section 68 or 95 of the 1989 Act (3.21, below).

Appropriation of land - adjustment of accounts

3.7   In line 7, for 'Section 101 of the Housing Finance Act 1972' read 'Paragraph 5 of Schedule 4 to the Local Government and Housing Act 1989'. In line 9, for 'Part V of the Housing Act 1957' read 'Part II of the Housing Act 1985'. The last sentence of the paragraph is no longer applicable.

Capital receipts

3.8-10 These paragraphs of the main text have been rendered obsolete by the Local Government and Housing Act 1989, Schedule 12 of which repealed section 27 of the Town and County Planning Act 1959 and the relevant paragraphs of Schedule 13 to the Local Government Act 1972. The application of capital receipts is now governed by sections 58 to 61 of the 1989 Act. Section 58 defines capital receipts to include not only sales of capital assets but also repayment of capital grants and advances made by the authority, and disposal of any investments other than those approved by the Secretary of State by regulations under section 66(1)(a) of the Act (currently the Local Authorities (Capital Finance) (Approved Investments) Regulations 1990, S.I. 1990/426). Section 59 requires local authorities to set aside a 'reserved' part of most capital receipts as 'provision to meet credit liabilities' (see 3.16, below). The reserved part is to be 75 per cent of receipts from sale of council houses and 50 per cent of other receipts (subs.(2)). These percentages may be altered by regulation (subs.(3)). Section 60 provides for the 'usable' balance of capital receipts to be applied, as the authority determine, either to meet capital expenditure or as provision to meet credit liabilities. Part VI of the Local Authorities (Capital Finance) Regulations 1990 (S.I. 1990/432) makes further detailed provision concerning capital receipts, including some variation of percentages under section 59(3) (reg.14). D.O.E. Circular 11/90, dated 2 August 1990, summarises the provisions of Act and regulations in some detail (Capital receipts are covered at Annex A, paras.43-64; likewise W.O. Circular 18/90, Annex A, paras.43-62).

Direct labour organisations

3.11   From 1 October 1989 the provisions of the Local Government, Planning and Land Act 1980 relating to direct labour organisations apply to authorities employing more than 15 persons in carrying out defined construction or maintenance work by direct labour, and separate accounts are required for each of the four categories of work specified in section 10 on which more than 15 persons are employed (Local Government (D.L.Os.) (Specified Number of Employed Persons) Order 1989, S.I. 1989/1589).

The provisions of section 13(2)(a) and 13(3), requiring a separate balance sheet for D.L.O. accounts, and those of section 16(4)-(6), requiring deficits to be charged first to any D.L.O. reserve fund and failing that to rate fund, were repealed by the Local Government Act 1988 (Sch.6, paras.5, 6).

Section 17 of the 1980 Act, relating to failure to produce the required rate of return on capital, was repealed by the Local Government Act 1988 (Sch.6, para.7) and replaced by new sections 19A and 19B inserted by the 1988 Act (Sch.6, para.9). Section 19A empowers the Secretary of State, if it appears to him that an authority have failed to produce the required rate of return on capital, or have not complied with other specified requirements of the legislation, to serve notice requiring them either to deny the breach complained of and justify the denial or to give reasons why he should not issue a direction under section 19B. That section empowers him to direct that the authority shall cease to have power to carry out specified work or that they shall have power to do so subject to complying with specified conditions.

3.11A Section 18 of the Local Government, Planning and Land Act 1980, as originally enacted, required local authorities to prepare and publish a report for each financial year on their direct labour work. New subsections inserted in this section by the Local Government Act 1988 (Sch.6, para.8) provided that the report should include a copy of the D.L.O. revenue account and a statement of rate of return (subs.(1A)), that a copy of the report should be sent to the Secretary of State and to the auditor by the following

31 October (subs.(2A)), and that the auditor should consider the statement of rate of return and give his written opinion on that statement to the authority and to the Secretary of State (subs.(2B)).

3.12   The decision of Nolan J. in *Wilkinson* v. *Doncaster M.B.C.* was upheld by the Court of Appeal, reported at (1985) 84 L.G.R. 257. The Court of Appeal held that 'building work', in the context, meant work of the type done by builders, and that painting work was clearly within that category.

Other direct service organisations

3.12A Part I of the Local Government Act 1988 requires local authorities and other public bodies who wish their staff to undertake defined activities to expose those activities to competitive tendering, and if successful to observe conditions relating to accounts, etc., similar to those applicable to direct labour organisations under the Local Government, Planning and Land Act 1980. The activities defined in the 1988 Act are refuse collection, cleaning of buildings, other cleaning, catering for purposes of schools and welfare, other catering, maintenance of grounds, and repair and maintenance of vehicles (s.2). The Secretary of State may add other activities to the list by order (s.2(3)), and has added management of sports and leisure facilities (L.G.A. 1988 (Competition in Sports and Leisure Facilities) Order 1989, S.I. 1989/2488). The Act provides for some exemptions, including emergency works (s.2(8)), and empowers the Secretary of State to make further exemptions by order (s.2(9)). Exemptions made by order include any defined activity for which expenditure in the previous year did not exceed £100,000 (Local Government Act 1988 (Defined Activities) (Exemptions) (England) Order 1988 (S.I. 1988/1372); likewise for Wales (S.I. 1988/1469).

3.12B A separate account is required for each defined activity which is subject to, and not exempted from, the requirements of the 1988 Act (s.9(2)). Amounts to be credited to the accounts in respect of work done are specified in section 9(3),(4). The Secretary of State may specify in writing other items to be entered in the accounts (s.9(5)). No other credits may be made in the accounts (s.9(6)). Section 10 requires authorities to secure that such financial objective as the Secretary of State may specify is met for each defined activity. Financial objectives for each defined activity have been specified in Annex A to D.O.E. Circular 19/88 (W.O. 39/88) as amended by D.O.E. letter of 27 March 1991 (W.O. 28.3.91), which requires a 5% rate of return on capital employed in each of the defined activities except building cleaning and management of sports and leisure facilities, where the objective is simply to break even. Section 11(2) requires authorities to prepare a report for each financial year on each defined activity, containing a summary revenue account which presents fairly the financial result of the work carried out and a statement showing whether the requirements of section 10 as to financial objectives have been met. A copy of the report is to be sent to the Secretary of State and the auditor by the following 31 October, and the auditor is to give his written opinion on the rate of return statement to the authority and to the Secretary of State (s.11(8)). Sections 13 and 14 contain provisions similar to those of sections 19A and 19B of the 1980 Act (3.11, above), enabling the Secretary of State, after due notice, to direct that the authority shall cease to have power to carry out specified work or that such power shall be subject to conditions.

3.12C The Chartered Institute of Public Finance and Accountancy has published a Code of Practice for Compulsory Competition which includes sections on revenue accounts; expenditure chargeable thereto; the accounting treatment of charges for work done by direct service organisation staff; the return on capital employed for direct service work; and reports on 1980 and 1988 Act work. This may evidently be considered as a 'generally recognised published code' for reference as to proper accounting practices under section 66(4) of the Local Government and Housing Act 1989 (4.50A, below).

Housing Revenue and Repairs Accounts

3.15   This paragraph should now read as follows:

'Every housing authority is required by section 74 of the Local Government and Housing Act 1989 to keep, in accordance with proper practices, a Housing Revenue Account recording the income and expenditure in respect of land, houses and other buildings provided under Part II of the Housing Act 1985, and of other houses and buildings specified in the section. The items to be included in the account are specified in detail in Schedule 4 to the 1989 Act, which includes wide powers for the Secretary of State to issue directions and determinations as to items in the accounts and to amend the Schedule by order. Major changes were made to the operation of the account by the 1989 Act, principally the ring-fencing of the account so that it became effectively a landlord's account with no general provision for contributions from general fund equivalent to the former rate fund contributions. Credit balances on the account may be transferred to other revenue accounts only by authorities to whom no Housing Revenue Account subsidy is payable for the year (Sch.4, Pt.III, para.2). Section 77 of the 1989 Act enables a housing authority to keep, in accordance with proper practices, a Housing Repairs Account, to be debited with expenditure on repairs and maintenance, and with such expenditure on improvement and replacement as the Secretary of State may determine. A Repairs Account, if opened, is to be credited with contributions from Housing Revenue Account and other sums receivable in connection with housing repairs and maintenance. The Repairs Account must not be allowed to fall into debit. The authority may carry some or all of any credit balance on the account to the credit of the Housing Revenue Account. Section 78 of the 1989 Act empowers the Secretary of State to give directions as to the accounting practices to be followed in the keeping of Housing Revenue and Repairs Accounts.'

Loans and Capital Finance

Loan redemption; Credit liabilities

3.16   The provisions of Schedule 13 to the Local Government Act 1972 described in paragraphs 3.16-18 were repealed by the Local Government and Housing Act 1989 (Sch.12). Part IV of that Act introduced a new regime for capital finance of local authorities. Provision for credit liabilities, that is, for loan redemption and other liabilities under 'credit arrangements' (such as leases and contracts providing for extended credit: s.48/1989) is now governed by sections 62-64 and Schedule 3, Parts III and IV, of the 1989 Act and Parts VII and VIII of the Local Authorities (Capital Finance) Regulations 1990 (S.I. 1990/432). Broadly speaking, section 63 and Schedule 3, Part IV, prescribe minimum revenue provision as the sum of an amount in respect of principal and an amount in respect of notional interest on credit arrangements.

The minimum revenue provision in respect of principal is based on percentages, prescribed in Part VIII of the above regulations, of the 'credit ceiling' of the authority at the end of the previous financial year. The credit ceiling, defined by section 62 and Schedule 3, Part III, is a measure of the difference between the total credit liabilities and the provision made to meet them; it corresponds in the former system to total outstanding loans fund advances.

The amount included in minimum revenue provision in respect of notional interest on credit arrangements is calculated, in general, by multiplying the cost of each credit arrangement by the discount rate applying when the credit arrangement was entered into or last varied. The cost of a credit arrangement is determined under section 49 of the 1989 Act and the discount rate is prescribed for each financial year by regulations made under that section (e.g., for 1991/2, the Local Authorities (Capital Finance) (Rate of Discount) Regulations 1991, S.I. 1991/97).

Section 64 provides that amounts set aside, either from revenue or from capital receipts, as provision for credit liabilities may be used to redeem debt or to meet liabilities under credit arrangements or as a substitute for new external borrowing authorised by ministerial credit approvals.

Detailed commentary on the above matters is contained in D.O.E. Circular 11/90 (in particular paras.32-39 and Annex A, paras.67-69; likewise W.O. Circular 18/90, paras.29-36 and Annex A, paras.65-77).

Loans funds

3.17   With the repeal of paragraph 15 of Schedule 13 to the 1972 Act (3.16, above), there is no requirement in the new system for local authorities to maintain loans funds. There is nothing to prevent them being maintained as accounts within the general or county fund, however. This is confirmed by D.O.E. Circular 11/90, which adds that it is expected that authorities will continue to charge their service revenue accounts for the use of capital assets (para.39; likewise W.O. Circular 18/90, para.36).

3.17A In *Stockdale* v. *Haringey L.B.C.*, [1989] R.A.107, the Court of Appeal upheld a declaration of the High Court, made on the application of the auditor, that the council had acted contrary to law in making advances in excess of borrowing powers from the loans fund to meet capital expenditure. The arguments in the case turned on the construction of provisions, now repealed, of Schedule 13 to the Local Government Act 1972. It appears that similar action by a council would be contrary to law under the new provisions, since capital expenditure not covered by ministerial credit approval must be charged to revenue account, and amounts set aside as provision to meet credit liabilities may be used to meet capital expenditure only if it is covered by such credit approval (Local Government and Housing Act 1989, ss.41, 42, 64).

Internal loans

3.18   The repeal of paragraphs 16 and 19 of Schedule 13 to the 1972 Act (3.16, above) renders this paragraph of the main text inoperative. Moreover any financial reserves maintained in place of former special funds (3.21, below) are part of the general or county fund, to which interest on internal balances will therefore fall to be credited. Special provisions apply, however, in respect of internal use of monies of superannuation and collection funds. Superannuation fund monies may be used by administering authorities for purposes covered by borrowing powers, interest being credited at a rate no lower than the current 7 day borrowing rate (Local Government Superannuation Regulations 1986, S.I. 1986/24, reg.P3(2), (3)). Collection fund monies may be transferred temporarily to general fund and retransferred together with interest at the 7 day London Interbank Offer Rate on the day of transfer from the collection fund (Collection Fund (England) Regulations 1989, S.I. 1989/2336, regs.11, 12; likewise for Wales, S.I. 1989/2363).

Publicity

3.20A Section 5(1) of the Local Government Act 1986 provides that a local authority shall keep a separate account of their expenditure on publicity. 'Publicity' is defined to refer to 'any communication, in whatever form, addressed to the public at large or to a section of the public' (s.6(4)). But section 5(5) empowers the Secretary of State to provide by order that section 5(1) does not apply to publicity or expenditure of a prescribed description. The Local Authorities (Publicity Account) (Exemption) Order 1987 (S.I. 1987/2004), made under this provision, exempts altogether authorities who resolve that their annual expenditure on publicity shall be less than £3000 and do keep below that figure. The order also exempts a number of heads of publicity. Any person interested may without payment inspect the account and make copies (s.5(2)). In guidance prepared in consultation with the Department of the Environment, the Chartered Institute of Public Finance and Accountancy has recommended that the publicity account should be operated as a memorandum account, costs being charged direct to services in the main accounts.

Special funds - financial reserves

3.21 The Local Government and Housing Act 1989, Schedule 12, repealed the provisions referred to in this paragraph of the main text. However, by Schedule 5, paragraphs 49 and 63, it introduced provisions, by way of amendment of sections 68 and 95 of the Local Government Finance Act 1988, requiring charging and precepting authorities to budget for financial reserves which the authority estimates it will be appropriate to raise to meet expenditure to be incurred and charged to a revenue account in any subsequent financial year (ss.68(4)(c),(4A)(b); 95(2)(c),(2A)(b)). These provisions appear to enable authorities to maintain reserves equivalent to the special funds established under the previous legislation, and as indicated at 3.6, above, section 41(2) of the 1989 Act apparently enables separate revenue accounts to be kept within the general fund or county fund for such reserves as the authority decide to maintain in accordance with section 68 or 95.

Superannuation funds

3.22 This paragraph should now read as follows:

'Superannuation funds must be maintained by administering authorities under the Local Government Superannuation Regulations 1986 (S.I. 1986/24), as amended, that is, county councils, London borough councils, the Common Council of the City of London, residuary bodies or district councils in whom funds are vested under section 60(1) or 66 of the Local Government Act 1985, the London Pensions Fund Authority (established by the London Government Reorganisation (Pensions etc.) Order 1989 (S.I. 1989/1815) to take over responsibility for the former fund of the Greater London Council) and the South Yorkshire Pensions Authority (established by the Local Government Reorganisation (Pensions etc.) (South Yorkshire) Order 1987 (S.I. 1987/2110). The financial arrangements between administering and employing authorities are set out in Part P of the regulations. Generally, all income and expenditure in respect of superannuation is credited and debited to the fund. Administering authorities may now charge administration expenses to the fund (reg.P2(2), inserted by the Local Government Superannuation (Amendment) Regulations 1989, S.I. 1989/371). Pensions increases under the Pensions (Increase) Act 1971 as amended, formerly chargeable to rate fund, are chargeable to the superannuation fund from 1 April 1990 (Local Government Superannuation (Funds etc.) Regulations 1990 (S.I. 1990/503). The additional cost of benefits resulting from certain discretionary powers of employing authorities, though borne by the fund in the first instance, are reimbursable by the employing authority (reg.P 9). Administering authorities are required to send to employing authorities, after audit, a copy of the revenue account and balance sheet of the fund and of any report of the auditor on his audit of the fund (reg.P4).'

III   ACCOUNTS OF OTHER BODIES

Health service bodies

3.24A Section 98(1) of the National Health Service Act 1977, as amended, provides that health service bodies, other than fund- holding practices, shall keep accounts in such form as the Secretary of State may with the approval of the Treasury direct. Section 98(2) requires those bodies to prepare and transmit to the Secretary of State annual accounts in such form as the Secretary of State may with the approval of the Treasury direct. District health authorities must include accounts of relevant community health councils (subs.(2A)). Section 98(2B), as inserted by paragraph 24 of Schedule 2 to the 1990 Act, provides that NHS trusts, in preparing such annual accounts, shall comply with any directions given by the Secretary of State with the approval of the Treasury as to the methods and principles according to which the accounts are to be prepared and the information given in the accounts. See also 3.59A- C, below.

3.24B Section 98(4) of the 1977 Act requires the Secretary of State to prepare, in such form as the Treasury may direct, annual summarised accounts of health bodies, other than fund-holding practices and the Dental Practice Board, and a statement of accounts of that Board containing such information as the Treasury may direct, and transmit them to the Comptroller and Audit General, who is required to examine and certify them and lay copies with his report before Parliament.

3.24C Section 98(2B) of the 1977 Act, as inserted by section 20(2) of the 1990 Act, provides that members of a fund-holding practice shall keep accounts and prepare annual accounts in respect of allotted sums in such form as the Secretary of State may with the approval of the Treasury direct, and that the annual accounts shall be submitted to the relevant family health services authority, which shall include a summarised version thereof in its own accounts.

IV   REGULATIONS RELATING TO ACCOUNTS

Accounts and Audit Regulations 1983

3.25 Section 23 of the Local Government Finance Act 1982, as amended, does not apply to health service bodies (National Health Service and Community Care Act 1990, Sch.4, para.13). Nor therefore do the Accounts and Audit Regulations made under that section.

3.26 In 1984 the Department of the Environment made proposals for new regulations which would have prescribed the form and content of local authority statements of accounts. The proposals were opposed by the Audit Commission and the Consultative Committee of Accountancy Bodies as unnecessary and unlikely to achieve their stated objectives, and in February 1986 it was announced that the Government had concluded that it should not proceed with the proposed regulations but had instead invited the local authority associations, in conjunction with the Audit Commission and the professional accountancy bodies, to establish their own arrangements for securing further improvement - including greater standardisation in local authority accounts. This object was achieved in the form of a Code of Practice on Local Authority Accounting issued in 1987 and revised with effect from 1 April 1990 (4.62A, below).

The 1983 Regulations were amended to a small extent by the Accounts and Audit (Amendment) Regulations 1986 and 1990 (S.Is. 1986/1271 and 1990/435) in order to reflect the abolition of some authorities and the creation of others, and to remove minor inconsistencies and inaccuracies.

No other changes have been made as a result of review as proposed in D.O.E. Circular 26/83 and noted in detail at paragraphs 3.31, 3.32, 3.38, 3.39, 3.41, 3.43, 3.44 and 3.45 of the main text.

The responsible financial officer

3.29   The Local Government Finance Act 1988 places new responsibilities, in the field of illegality etc., on the officer responsible for financial administration under section 151 of the Local Government Act 1972, who is referred to in the 1988 Act as the chief finance officer of the authority (6.40A-C, below).

Statements of accounts

3.41   Amendments to regulation 7 by the Accounts and Audit (Amendment) Regulations 1986 and 1990 (S.Is. 1986/1271 and 1990/435) apply the requirements as to preparation of statements of accounts to joint authorities established by the Local Government Act 1985, authorities established by the Waste Regulation and Disposal (Authorities) Order 1985 (S.I. 1985/1884), and the Broads Authority.

3.43   As to inspection and copying of immediate reports made during an audit, see 4.104-5, 4.110A, App.E.2, below.

Enforcement of regulations by mandamus

3.52, n.16 For 'pp.643-4' of *Wade* read '(6th edn.) pp.660-1'.

3.53   For 'p.642' of *Wade* read '(6th edn.) p.698'.

3.54   For 'p.578' of *Wade* read '(6th edn.) p.701'.

Health service bodies

3.59A Section 99 of the National Health Service Act 1977 authorises the Secretary of State to make regulations relating to authorisation of payments by health service bodies and other financial arrangements (subss.(1), (2)). Subsection (3) authorises the giving of directions to any of the bodies on any matter with respect to which regulations may be made under the section. The Secretary of State may also issue directions to health service bodies under sections 97A and 97B of the 1977 Act relating to the bodies' financial duties and under section 98(2) relating to the form of their accounts.

3.59B No regulations have been made under section 99, but general directions under that section on financial control and under section 97A on financial planning and monitoring, and on the definition of attributable expenditure for the purposes of cash limits, have been issued by the Department of Health as an annex to Health Circular

HC(91)25 dated May 1991. The directions on financial control include a requirement for the immediate notification to the auditor of all suspected cases of fraud (Sch.3, para. 1n.)

3.59C Directions under section 98(2) in respect of the preparation and transmission to the Secretary of State of annual accounts have been issued as enclosures to Health Circulars HC(86)12 dated December 1986 and HC(FP)(87)(1) dated March 1987 (in Wales, WHC(86)67 and WHC(FP)(85)17). These circulars also required health service bodies to implement the detailed accounting arrangements set out in a National Health Service Manual for Accounts.

CHAPTER 4

GENERAL POWERS AND DUTIES OF THE AUDITOR

I DUTIES COMMON TO ALL AUDITORS

Duty of professional care

Comparison of local government/health and company auditors

4.4   In *Jones* v. *Department of Employment*, [1989] Q.B.1, the plaintiff brought an action against the Department alleging negligence by its employee, a social security adjudication officer, whose disallowance of the plaintiff's claim for benefit had been reversed on appeal. The Court of Appeal held that the officer did not attract immunity of a judicial nature because he was performing an administrative function, but that he was not under a duty of care to the plaintiff, and therefore not liable for negligence, because his duty lay in the field of public law. Therefore, misfeasance apart, his decisions were susceptible to challenge only by judicial review and by statutory appeal procedure. It may be considered that this reasoning would apply to the local government/health services auditor, even in respect of his general duties under section 15 of the 1982 Act.

4.4,n.1 For 'p.676' of *Wade* read '(6th edn.,), p.785'.

4.5   Section 333 of the Companies Act 1948 has been replaced by the similar provisions of section 212 of the Insolvency Act 1986.

4.5,n.2 For '4th edn., Vol.7, 1196' of *Halsbury,* read '4th edn., (Reissue), Vol.7, 1690'.

4.6   In lines 5-6, for 'Section 14 of the Companies Act 1967' read 'Section 235 of the Companies Act 1985, as substituted by section 9 of the Companies Act 1989'.

4.7   In line 10, for 'para.21' read 'para.43/1990'. In line 11, for 'guidance notes', read 'the *Code of Practice on Local Authority Accounting*'. In line 12, for 'App., para.2(a)', read 'para. 24(a)/1990'.

Local government/health auditors - Code of Audit Practice

4.10   In line 5, for 'para.9' read 'para.12/1990' (but the reference to 'the responsibilities of joint auditors' does not appear in the 1990 edition). In lines 6 and 7 for 'the Commission's basic philosophy (para.6)', read 'the Commission's basic approach (para.8/1990)'. In line 9, for 'para.32', read 'para.16/1990'. The 1990 Code does not refer to the CIPFA Report on Standards mentioned in lines 9 to 11, but itself includes detailed comments on the application of the Auditors' Operational Standard to audits covered by the Code (paras.17-23/1990).

Cases on duties of company auditors

4.18   Subsequent cases have made it clear that in cases of negligent misstatement, for example in audit reports, foreseeability that the plaintiff would rely upon the statement is a necessary but not a sufficient condition for liability; it is also necessary to establish a relationship between the parties sufficiently proximate to create a duty of care from one to the other and it must be just and reasonable to impose such a duty of care. In *Al Saudi Banque* v. *Clarke Pixley*, [1990] Ch. 313, a bank which had made loans to a company which proved to be insolvent alleged that they had relied on the auditors' report and sued them for negligence. It was held that the test of proximity was not satisfied and that it would not be just and reasonable to impose a duty of care. In *Caparo Industries* v. *Dickman*, [1990] 2 A.C. 605, the House of Lords held that the auditors' relationship with shareholders does not give rise to a duty of care to individual shareholders as potential purchasers of further shares; so shareholders who, relying on negligently prepared accounts, purchase more shares and suffer loss have no claim in negligence against the auditors. See also *James McNaughton Paper Group Ltd* v. *Hicks Anderson & Co*, [1991] 2 Q.B. 113.

4.24   In the 1990 Code of Audit Practice the section on responsibilities of the auditor in relation to fraud (now at paras.27-29) is extended to cover 'fraud and irregularities', defined to refer to 'intentional distortion of financial statements and accounting records and to misappropriation of assets, whether or not accompanied by distortion of financial statements and accounting records' (para.27). A new paragraph is inserted stating that the primary responsibility for the prevention and detection of fraud and irregularities rests with management (para.28), but the statement of the auditor's special responsibilities is repeated without significant change (para.29), as is that of his responsibilities in relation to corruption (paras.30-33).

II   GENERAL DUTIES OF LOCAL GOVERNMENT/HEALTH AUDITORS

Audit requirements in the public sector

4.26   In line 2, for 'para.6(a)' read 'para.8(a)/1990'.

The Code of Audit Practice

4.38   Section 14 of the 1982 Act was amended by the National Health Service and Community Care Act 1990 (s.20, Sch.4, para.4) to provide that a different code could be prepared for the audit of health service bodies (subs.(1)) and that organisations connected with the health service should be consulted before the preparation or alteration of such a code or of a code covering both local government and health service audit (subs.(7)).

4.39   The 1983 Code referred to in this paragraph has now been superseded (4.39A to 4.39C, below).

4.39A In accordance with section 14(3) of the Local Government Finance Act 1982 a revised Code of Local Government Audit Practice was approved by each House of Parliament and came into force in February 1988. Additions to the Code were subsequently required by the enactment, in the Local Government Act 1988, of new powers for the auditor to issue prohibition orders and to apply for judicial review. These additions were effected by the Commission under section 14(4) of the 1982 Act, and the Code thus further revised came into force in July 1988. Further revision was necessitated in 1990 by the extension of the 1982 Act provisions to health service audit, and the latest revised Code of Audit Practice for England and Wales, covering both local government and health service audit, was approved by both Houses of Parliament and came into effect on 28 November 1990. References in this supplement to paragraphs of the Code followed by the suffix '/1990' are to the 1990 edition of the Code, which is reproduced at Appendix C, below.

4.39B The introduction to the revised Code indicates that it draws upon *The Auditing Standards and Guidelines* (as did the earlier codes) and the Auditing Guidelines *Applicability to the Public Sector of Auditing Standards and Guidelines* and *The Impact of Regulations on Public Sector Audits,* developed by the Auditing Practices Committee of the Consultative Committee of the Accountancy Bodies (para.3/1990). Paragraph 5 of the 1990 Code repeats the emphasis of paragraph 4 of the 1983 Code that the auditor is expected to discharge his professional responsibilities independently, both of the Commission and its officers and of the authority. Paragraph 6, which did not appear in the 1983 Code, points out that aspects of the Code may be inappropriate to the audit of certain bodies, in particular small bodies such as parish councils, parish meetings, community councils and internal drainage boards, and in the health service, practice fund holders and special trustees. Such bodies are referred to as 'non-principal' authorities.

4.39C The arrangement of the 1990 Code is somewhat different to that of the 1983 Code. Its main provisions are now in five parts. The first sets out the general duties and objectives of auditors under the 1982 Act and refers to the requirements placed on the auditor by the 'basic approach' of the Commission and by considerations of independence and due professional care. The second part relates to the detailed planning and conduct of the audit and summarises the auditor's particular responsibilities with respect to fraud and irregularities, corruption, legality and value for money. The third part deals with the auditor's reporting responsibilities, including the report in the public interest under section 15(3), management letters to members on matters arising at the audit, and the auditor's certificate and opinion on the statement of accounts under section 18. (The Appendix to the Code gives examples of the forms of certificate and opinion). The fourth part of the Code covers the particular responsibilities of local government auditors: the exercise of powers under the 1982 Act relating to illegality (s.19); wilful misconduct and failure to bring into account (s.20); prohibition orders (s.25A); application for judicial review (s.25D); and the response to questions and objections by local government electors under section 17 of the Act. The fifth part refers to the specific responsibilities of health service auditors. The terms 'local authorities' and 'health authorities' in the Code refer respectively to all local government bodies and health service bodies subject to audit under the 1982 Act (para.7).

Government grants and contracts etc.

4.45,n.9 Individual variations have subsequently been made to the list of claims which are to be certified by an auditor appointed by the Commission.

4.45A The Local Government Finance Act 1988 (s.137, Sch.12, para.3(4),(5)) inserted a new paragraph (c) in section 29(1) of the 1982 Act requiring the Commission, if so required by the body concerned, to make arrangements for certifying the body's calculation of its non-domestic rating contribution under paragraph 5(6)(b) of Schedule 8 to the 1988 Act.

4.45B The Local Government and Housing Act 1989 (s.184(2)) extended section 29(1)(a) of the 1982 Act to cover certification of claims and returns in respect of grants by 'public authorities', and inserted a new paragraph (d) in section 29(1) applying the section to certification of any return where audit certification is required or authorised by statute. 'Public authority' is defined for this purpose to mean 'a body established by or under the Treaties or by or under any enactment'. 'The Treaties' means treaties relating to the European Communities as defined in detail in Schedule 1 to the European Communities Act 1972 (Interpretation Act 1978, Sch.1). Full cost must be charged for certification under paragraphs (c) and (d) of section 29(1) (s.29(5)).

4.45C Section 29(1) is applicable to 'any body whose accounts are required to be audited in accordance with this Part of this Act' and is therefore applicable to health service bodies.

III PREPARATION OF ACCOUNTS

Compliance with statutory requirements

4.47A Section 23 of the 1982 Act is not applicable to health service bodies and hence the 1983 Regulations do not apply to them. Section 15(1)(a) is amended by the National Health Service and Community Care Act 1990 (Sch.4, para.5) to provide that the auditor of a health service body must satisfy himself that accounts are prepared (in place of the reference to regulations) in accordance with directions under the National Health Service Act 1977, section 98(2) or (2B); these are directions of the Secretary of State relating to the form of the accounts of health service bodies (3.24A,C, above; it appears that s.15(1)(a) applies to both subss.(2B) of s.98, as inserted by para.24, Sch.2/1990 and s.20(2)/1990 respectively).

4.48   In respect of health service bodies, for the reference to section 19 of the 1982 Act read section 20(3) of the 1990 Act (5.6 B-C, below).

Proper accounting practices

4.50   In line 7, for 'paragraph 6(a)', read 'paragraph 8(a)/1990'. In line 15, for 'para.21', read 'para.43/1990'.

4.50A 'Proper practices', for the purposes of the Local Government Finance Act 1982 and subsequent (including future) enactments, were defined in relation to local authorities by the Local Government and Housing Act 1989 (s.66(4),(5)) to mean accounting practices which the authority are required to follow by enactment or which, whether by reference to any generally recognised published code or otherwise, are regarded as proper accounting practices to be followed by local authorities and are not in conflict with statute. The definition applies only to local authorities (as defined in s.39/1989), and therefore not to health service bodies.

D.O.E. Circular 11/90 and W.O. Circular 18/90 draw attention to this definition in Annex D. They also refer to statutory proper practices relating to capital in Part IV of the 1989 Act, (3.2C, 3.8-10, 3.16, above) and to non-statutory proper practices to be found in the Statement of Recommended Practice and the Code of Practice referred to at 4.55 and 4.62A, below.

Fairness of apportionments

4.51   The example given of application to housing rents must be read as subject to the changes of law relating to the Housing Revenue Account mentioned at 3.15, above.

Accounting standards

4.54   New arrangements for the setting of accounting standards came into operation on 1 August 1990. There is now an independent Accounting Standards Board (ASB) which sets standards in its own right without requiring approval from the Consultative Committee of Accountancy Bodies. It receives guidance from a Financial Reporting Council with membership drawn from a wide constituency of interests including accountancy firms, business, banking and central and local government. An Urgent Issue Task Force, an off-shoot of the ASB, is able to make pronouncements on recommended practice without seeking consultation. An independent Review Panel examines contentious departures from accounting standards.

4.55   In recent years the former Accounting Standards Committee (ASC) had developed a system of Statements of Recommended Practice (SORPs) which were not mandatory on members of the accountancy bodies but which relevant entities were encouraged to follow. Some SORPs were developed and issued by the ASC itself. Others, referred to as 'franked SORPs' were developed by 'industry groups' and issued after approval by the ASC. The CIPFA guidance notes referred to in the main text, 4.55-60, were superseded in 1986 by a franked SORP applicable to local authorities in England and Wales and this was replaced in 1990 by a franked SORP on *The Application of SSAPs to Local Authorities in Great Britain.*

4.56   For 'guidance notes', in last line, read 'SORP'.

4.57   With the exception of SSAP 16, which was withdrawn in April 1988, all the SSAPs listed in the main text remain applicable (in some cases as revised) and are covered in the current SORP referred to above. The same applies to the following new SSAPS:

SSAP 20 – Foreign currency translation

SSAP 21 – Accounting for leases and hire purchase contracts

The SORP indicates that SSAPs 22 and 23 are not applicable to local authorities. A statement on the applicability of SSAP 24 - Accounting for pension costs - is under consideration. All extant SSAPs were adopted by the Accounting Standards Board at its first meeting, but it is understood that they are to be reviewed in detail in due course and may be replaced by new Financial Reporting Standards.

4.57A The ASC itself issued in May 1986 SORP 1 - Pension scheme accounts. This relates to the accounts of pension schemes themselves, as opposed to SSAP 24 which relates to accounting for pensions costs in the accounts of employers. *The Code of Practice on Local Authority Accounting* (4.62A, below) provides that financial statements of local authority superannuation fund accounts shall be prepared in accordance with the recommendations of SORP 1, but with limited disclosure requirements (Part 5(iii), heading 'Superannuation Fund Accounts').

4.60   The SORP noted at 4.55 above takes broadly the same line as the former guidance note on the matters referred to in this paragraph.

4.61   The judgment as to failure to observe proper practices by local authorities must now be made in the light of the definition of 'proper practices' in the Local Government and Housing Act 1989 (4.50A, above). As to materiality, see 4.64, 4.67, below.

Health service bodies

4.61A A statement of Accounting Standards for health authorities is expected to be approved shortly and issued by the Secretary of State, to take effect from financial year 1991-92, revising and replacing previous standards in operation from 1983-84.

Standard form of accounts - Code of Practice on Local Authority Accounting

4.62   In 1985 CIPFA issued a new recommended standard form of revenue accounts comprising a subjective analysis into standard groupings and sub-groups common to all services, termed the 1985 *Standard Classification*, and an objective analysis into services and divisions thereof, presented in service guidance booklets. This was supplemented in 1986 by a further CIPFA publication, the *Local Authority Accounting Manual*, which brought together all CIPFA's accounting recommendations in one volume. The 1985 *Standard Classification* was amended in 1988.

4.62A In June 1987 CIPFA issued a *Code of Practice on Local Authority Accounting* which had been prepared by a joint CIPFA – Audit Commission working party. It followed an invitation from the Minister for Local Government to the local authority associations to formulate – in conjunction with the accounting bodies and the Audit Commission – their own proposals for securing improvements in local authority accounting practice; these proposals would then provide an alternative to a major statutory extension to the Accounts and Audit Regulations. The Code was adopted by the local authority associations and was subsequently franked by the Accounting Standards Committee as a Statement of Recommended Practice. A revised Code of Practice under the title *Code of Practice in Local Authority Accounting for Great Britain* has now been issued to have effect for financial years commencing 1 April 1990.

4.62B The Introduction to the Local Authority Accounting Code states that it applies formally in England and Wales to local authorities, joint committees, joint boards of principal authorities, police and fire authorities and residuary bodies, and specifies the principles and practices of accounting required to prepare a statement of accounts which presents fairly the financial position and transactions of an authority. It does not apply formally to parish, town and community councils, but states that its provisions may be relevant to them and may be taken into account when statements of accounts are prepared by them. The Introduction also states that it is supported by a number of detailed accounting recommendations in primary sources set out in the Appendix to the Code. These include the 1985 *Standard Classification* as amended, the 1986 *Local Authority Accounting Manual* referred to at 4.62, above, and the SORP on the *Application of SSAPs to Local Authorities in Great Britain* (4.55, above).

The auditor's certificate and opinion on the accounts

4.63   Paragraph 42 of the 1990 Code of Audit Practice requires that the auditor's certificate should identify the accounts for the financial year to which the certificate of audit completion relates and that the certificate should refer expressly to the fact that the audit has been completed in accordance with Part III of the Local Government Finance Act 1982 in the case of local authorities and, in the case of health authorities, in accordance with Part I of the National Health Service and Community Care Act 1990, which amended Part III of the 1982 Act. Paragraph 44 indicates that for non-principal authorities (4.39B, above), who are not required to prepare statements of accounts, audit opinions may be varied in recognition that accounting conventions relevant to principal authorities may not be applicable, as illustrated in the Appendix to the Code.

4.63A For health authorities, the audit opinion is given on a preprinted standard set of forms prepared by the Department of Health or Welsh Office. The set of forms includes the financial statements of trust funds, on which the auditor is required to give a separate opinion, also provided for on the forms.

4.64   This paragraph should now read as follows:

'The 1990 Code of Audit Practice requires the auditor to state expressly in his opinion whether the audit has been completed in accordance with the Code of Audit Practice and whether the statement of accounts presents fairly the financial position of the authority at 31 March and its income and expenditure for the year then ended (para.43). Paragraphs 45-6 of the Code set out detailed requirements concerning auditors' opinions on statements of accounts, and the Appendix thereto sets out forms of certificate and opinion which auditors should adopt, with examples (para.56). Where an auditor has issued a report in the public interest in the course of or at the conclusion of the audit, this fact should be referred to in the certificate and opinion (para.48). Paragraphs 24 and 25 of the Code require that the auditor should satisfy himself about specified matters in relation to the statement, and if not satisfied on such matters which are material to the statement, should qualify his opinion. A matter is to be judged material if knowledge of it would be likely to influence the general impression of the authority's financial position formed by a user of the statement (para.53). Any qualification should be reported to the authority under section 15(3) of the 1982 Act with any requisite explanations (para.52). A copy of any qualified opinion should be sent to the Audit Commission, and in the case of a health authority also to the Secretary of State (para.55).'

4.65   This paragraph should now read as follows:

'The first of the specified matters on which the auditor is to satisfy himself is compliance with the *Code of Practice on Local Authority Accounting* issued by CIPFA or the Accounting Standards for health authorities issued and approved by the Secretary of State (4.62A, 4.61A, above), except where compliance would be impracticable, misleading or otherwise inappropriate (para.24(a), (c)). For accounting policies not covered by the CIPFA Code or NHS Accounting Standards which have a material effect, the auditor must be satisfied that the policies are appropriate to the circumstances of the authority and comply with good practice (para.24(b),(d)). Similarly he must be satisfied that the figures in the statement of accounts are substantially correct; that descriptions are unambiguous and not misleading; that the accounts comply with statutory and other requirements applicable to them; that there is adequate disclosure of all appropriate items; and that information is suitably classified and presented (para.24(e)- (i)).'

4.66   In line 1, for 'paragraph 9 of the Appendix to the Code' read 'Paragraph 49 of the 1990 Code'. In line 2, after 'delayed', insert 'e.g.'. In line 6, for 'Attachment' read 'Appendix'.

4.66A As to the auditor's duty under the Local Government Act 1988 to give his written opinion on rate of return statements of direct labour and direct service organisations, see 3.11A and 3.12B, above.

The auditor's remedies

4.67   In line 7, for 'guidance notes on accounting standards' read 'the CIPFA *Code of Practice on Local Authority Accounting* or the Accounting Standards for health authorities issued by the Secretary of State' (see 4.61A, 4.62A, above). In line 8, for 'paragraph 2 of the Appendix to the Code' read 'paragraph 24 of the 1990 Code'.

4.68-70 For references to paragraph 2 of the Appendix to the Code substitute references to paragraph 24 of the 1990 Code.

4.69-70 In the light of the definition of 'proper practices' in section 66(4) and (5) of the Local Government and Housing Act 1989 (4.50A, above), it now apparently follows that a material departure from applicable accounting standards or other criteria of the Code of Audit Practice would amount to a failure to observe proper practices in the compilation of the accounts within the meaning of section 15(1)(b) of the Local Government Finance Act 1982. As to materiality, it is to be noted that the Explanatory Foreword to the SORP on the *Application of Accounting Standards to Local Authorities in Great Britain* states that 'This SORP need not be applied to items the effect of which is judged to be immaterial to an understanding of the financial statements'; and that the *Code of Practice on Local Authority Accounting* states that 'strict compliance with this Code, both as to disclosure and accounting principles, is not necessary where the amounts involved are not material to the fair presentation of the financial position of the authority and to an understanding of the statement of accounts by a reader' (Pt.3, para.7). It therefore appears that non-compliance which was not material in this sense would not necessarily amount to a failure to observe proper practices as defined by section 66 of the 1989 Act, since the 'generally recognised published codes' do not require compliance in these circumstances.

4.70,n.14 Powers of the Secretary of State to issue directions in respect of housing accounts now appear in the Local Government and Housing Act 1989: s.78, Sch.4.

IV ECONOMY, EFFICIENCY AND EFFECTIVENESS

The auditor's duty

4.72   In line 4, for 'paragraph 40' read 'paragraph 35/1990'.

4.74   In line 9, for 'paragraphs 41-4' read 'paragraphs 36-40/1990'.

4.75   In lines 5/6, for 'paragraph 24 of the 1983 Code' read 'paragraph 58 of the 1990 Code'. In lines 8 and 10, for 'sub-paragraphs (b) and (c)' read 'sub-paragraphs (f)and (g)'.

4.77A In order to remove misunderstanding of the interrelationship and differences between value for money audit work and the legality functions of the auditor, and to clarify the issue, the Audit Commission in 1986 obtained legal advice and circulated a summary of the salient points as follows:

'*Section 19, Local Government Finance Act 1982*

If an authority failed to take action to avoid loss through wasteful expenditure identified in an audit report, it would be a matter for consideration whether action could be taken under section 19 for a declaration that such expenditure was unlawful and for an order for repayment.

Applying previous judgments, it is clear that the auditor could not take section 19 action on the ground solely that an authority had failed to take action to avoid loss due to expenditure which he considered he had identified in a previous report as wasteful. Nor would it be sufficient for him to convince the court that the expenditure was wasteful. That would be necessary in the first place. But as shown by previous cases, the court will not substitute its own opinion for that of the authority unless it is satisfied that the authority has abused its discretion. It would, therefore, be necessary also for the auditor to convince the court on this point, and, for that purpose, to produce clear and compelling evidence to satisfy the court that the authority, in failing to eliminate the waste in question, had acted or failed to act for an ulterior purpose or in a way in which no reasonable authority could have done.

Section 20, Local Government Finance Act 1982

It is clear that the auditor could not certify a sum as due from members of an authority solely on the ground that the authority had failed to take action to avoid loss which he considered he had identified in a previous report as loss through waste. He would need evidence adequate to satisfy himself (and to defend his decision to the satisfaction of the court, if necessary), that in failing to take action to avoid such loss, the members concerned had deliberately decided on a course which they knew to be wrong or as to which they were recklessly indifferent whether it was wrong or not. He would also need evidence to establish, and to defend his decision to the satisfaction of the court, that the knowingly or recklessly wrongful conduct of the members had caused loss of the amount certified due.

Conclusion

Under both sections 19 and 20 there are thus strict and heavy conditions to be satisfied before an auditor could take action in respect of failure to avoid loss due to waste, even though he had referred to the matter in a previous report. Such attention would be unlikely to succeed, for example, in cases where there was any scope for a reasonable man to differ from the auditor's opinion that there was loss due to waste, or where the failure to take action was due to negligence which could not be proved to be deliberate. It would be only in blatant cases of provable wrongful or irrational behaviour, as more closely defined above, that there would be any likelihood of such action succeeding.'

Studies by the Audit Commission

4.78   Amendments to section 26 of the 1982 Act by the National Health Service and Community Care Act 1990 provide that before undertaking a study of a health service body under the section the Commission shall consult the Secretary of State and the Comptroller and Auditor General; and that the latter shall be supplied, on request, with all material relating to such a study (Sch.4, para.18). Section 29(2) was also amended by the 1990 Act to authorise a health service body, instead of consulting associations of employees, to consult such other organisations as appear to the body to be appropriate (Sch.4, para.20).

4.79   The last sentence of this paragraph is no longer applicable; the requirement of paragraph 44 of the 1983 Code does not appear in the 1990 Code.

Studies under section 27 may not be applied to health service bodies. Studies of such bodies under section 26 may take account of the impact of statutory provisions and directions or guidance by the Secretary of State but the merits of his policy objectives may not be questioned (National Health Service and Community Care Act 1990, Sch.4, para.19). See also 4.93A, below.

V THE AUDITOR'S REPORT

4.83   In line 9, for 'Companies Act 1967, s.14', read 'Companies Act 1985, s.235, as substituted by Companies Act 1989, s.9'.

Contents of the report

4.85   In line 17, for 'paragraph 26' read 'paragraph 60/1990'.

4.86   This paragraph should now read as follows:

'Paragraph 58 of the 1990 Code of Audit Practice lists examples of matters which, if significant, would call for a report:

(a)   The fact that the auditor's opinion on the statement of accounts has been qualified, and conclusions therefrom.

(b)   Delayed preparation of accounts.

(c)   Failure to comply with statutory requirements.

(d)   Excessive or inadequate levels of balances, inappropriate levels of provisions, lack of prudence, prospective budget deficits, and other similar financial matters calling for comment.

(e)   Lack of action on matters previously reported by the auditor, including previously identified value for money opportunities.

(f)   Absence of or weaknesses in arrangements for securing economy, efficiency and effectiveness in the use of resources.

(g)   Unnecessary expenditure or loss of income due to waste, extravagance, inefficient financial administration, poor value for money, mistake or other cause.

(h)   Weaknesses in management information systems and monitoring arrangements.

(i)   High levels of arrears, deficiencies in income collection procedures.

(j)   Deficiencies in internal control arrangements (including internal audit).

(k)   Objections received at the audit of local authorities and action under sections 19, 20, 25A and 25D of the Act.

(l)   Misconduct, frauds, or special investigations.

The list does not purport to be exhaustive, but it shows the wide extent of the auditor's duty of report.'

4.87   In lines 1, 6, 7 and 10, for 'paragraphs 25-29' read 'paragraphs 59-63/1990'.

4.88   In line 2, for 'paragraph 26' read 'paragraph 60/1990'. In line 3, for 'his' read 'an'. In line 4, for 'councils' read 'authorities'.

Policy and administration

4.90   In line 1 on page 97, for 'paragraphs 24(c) and 26' read 'paragraphs 58(g) and 60/1990'.

4.92   The first sentence of this paragraph should now read as follows:

'Paragraph 39 of the 1990 Code of Practice states:

"It is not the auditor's function to question policy. There is, however, a responsibility, particularly in the audit of local authorities, to consider the effects of policy and to examine the arrangements by which policy decisions are reached"'.

4.93   The last two sentences of this paragraph should now read as follows:

'If paragraph 39 of the 1990 Code is read as a whole and in the context of the whole Code it is clearly not intended to run counter to this statement of law. This appears both from what is said in that paragraph on the auditor's responsibilities in the policy area and also from comparison with paragraph 60 of the 1990 Code, which contains the clear statement of the true limitation on the auditor's function as set out at 4.88, above.'

4.93A As regards health authorities, paragraph 40 of the 1990 Code states that it is not for the auditor to question overall policy objectives determined by the Secretary of State but indicates that the auditor should review local implementation of policy to ensure consistency with approved objectives and due authorisation. See also 4.79, above.

The Auditor's report – procedure

4.94   A copy of the auditor's report on a health service body must be sent to the Secretary of State as to the Commission (s.18(4)/1982, as amended by the National Health Service and Community Care Act 1990, Sch.4, para.8). Copies of reports on district and family health service authorities in England are also to be sent to regional health authorities (Code of Audit Practice 1990, para.57).

Consideration of the report

4.101   The reasoning in this paragraph receives some support from *R.* v. *Brent L.B.C., ex parte Gladbaum* (1989), 88 L.G.R. 627, in which it was held that a council could not delegate its power to appoint and remove members of committees for the reason, *inter alia*, that Parliament could not have intended that power to be delegated under section 101 of the 1972 Act, which authorised delegation not only to committees but to officers and other local authorities.

4.102   The provisions of Part VA of the 1972 Act as to publicity for reports (4.103, below) apply also to committees and sub-committees of principal councils (s.100E(1)).

Section 100 of the 1972 Act does not apply to health authorities, but the 1960 Act itself applies to committees of such authorities to whom the Act applies (4.103, below) which include all the members of the body (s.2).

Publicity for the report

Availability to press and public

4.103   The Public Bodies (Admission to Meetings) Act 1960 does not now apply to principal councils, for which it was replaced by Part VA of the Local Government Act 1972, inserted by the Local Government (Access to Information) Act 1985. The new provisions repeated those of section 1(4)(b) of the 1960 Act relating to the supply to newspapers of agenda, reports and other related documents (s.100B(7)). They also provided that such documents should be available to members of the public before a meeting (s.100B(1) and that minutes, reports and other related documents should be available to members of the public after a meeting (s.100C(1)). In each case there is provision for availability to be restricted in respect of material relating to items during which the meeting is likely to be, or was, not open to the public (ss.100B(2),(8), 100C(1)). But section 18(5) of the Local Government Finance Act 1982 was amended by the 1985 Act (Sch.2, para.7) to secure that auditors' reports should be compulsorily available to press and public, even though dealt with in a period of a meeting during which the public was excluded.

The operation of section 18(5) is not affected by section 18A of the 1982 Act, which introduced wider provisions in respect of publicity for immediate reports made during the course of local government audit (4.110A, below).

The 1960 Act remains in force for parochial authorities. It also applies to regional health authorities, district health authorities and family health service authorities, and to special health authorities for which the establishing order so provides. The original text of 4.103 therefore applies to such bodies (except as to committees of health authorities: 4.102, above).

4.104 Section 24 of the 1982 Act does not apply to health service bodies (Sch.4/1990, para.14). Nor does it apply to immediate reports made during the course of a local government audit (Local Government (Publicity for Auditors' Reports) Act 1991, s.1(3)), for which wider provisions in respect of publicity are now contained in section 18A of the 1982 Act (4.110A, below).

4.105 The Accounts and Audit (Amendment) Regulations 1986 (S.I. 1986/1271) amended regulation 14 in respect of notices required for parochial authorities. Where the auditor makes a report at the close of an audit, the requirements remain the same as stated in the main text, but the reference in line 12 is now to regulation 6A. Where there is no report all parochial authorities, whatever their population, have the option of giving notice in a conspicuous place of the conclusion of the audit (reg.6, as substituted by the 1986 Regulations).

For immediate reports to local authorities during an audit regulation 14 appears no longer applicable, since the rights of local government electors to inspect reports, to which the regulation refers, do not now apply in respect of immediate reports (4.104, above). As to publicity now for such reports, see 4.110A, below.

The 1983 Regulations do not apply to health service bodies (Sch.4/1990, para.13).

Enforcement of publicity provisions

4.109 Intentional obstruction or refusal to comply with the provisions of sections 100B and 100C of the Local Government Act 1972, noted at 4.103, above, is an offence punishable on summary conviction by a fine not exceeding level 1 on the standard scale (s.100H(4)). The maximum fine on level 1 is currently £50 (Criminal Penalties etc. (Increase) Order 1984, S.I. 1984/447).

Immediate reports - additional publicity

4.110A Further provision in respect of these matters is now made by section 18A of the Local Government Finance Act 1982, inserted by the Local Government Finance (Publicity for Auditors' Reports) Act 1991, which applies only to 'immediate' reports made under section 15(3) of the 1982 Act during the course of a local government audit, not to reports made at the conclusion of an audit. The body to whom an immediate report is made must supply a copy forthwith to every member of the body and must forthwith advertise in the local press, identifying the subject-matter of the report and stating that any member of the public may inspect and make copies of the report at specified times and places. Members of the public are also entitled to be supplied with copies on payment of a reasonable sum (subss.(1),(2); see App.E.2A, below, for a form of notice). Failure to comply with, or obstruction of, the above provisions involves liability to a fine of up to level 3 of the standard scale (subss.(3),(4)). An auditor may also notify the making of, or supply a copy of, any immediate report which he has made to any person he thinks fit (subs.(5)). Section 18A does not apply to a health service body (subs.(6)). Nor does it apply to any report sent before 27 August 1991 (ss.1(5), 2(2)/1991). The section does not affect the operation of section 18(5), as set out in paragraph 4.103, main text (subs.(7)).

Management letters

4.111 Paragraphs 64 and 65 of the 1990 Code of Audit Practice expand on the subject of management letters. Paragraph 64 provides that the draft management letter should be discussed with the officers concerned and will then provide the agenda for a meeting which the auditor should seek with appropriate members at which he can explain and amplify his concerns and respond to members' questions. It also provides that the letter in its final form should be sent to all members, by the auditor himself if necessary, and that in addition to the copy to the Commission copies of letters to health authorities are to be sent to the Secretary of State, or in the case of English district and family health service authorities to the appropriate regional health authority. Paragraph 65 indicates that the letter should be sent by 31 December following the end of the relevant financial year, save in exceptional circumstances.

VI POWERS AS TO DOCUMENTS AND INFORMATION

4.112 Section 16(1) of the Local Government Finance Act 1982 was amended by the Local Government Act 1988 (s.30(2)) to replace the words 'for the purposes of the audit' by 'for the purposes of his functions under this Act'. This was presumably deemed necessary to remove any doubt whether the auditor's rights to obtain documents and information extended to cover the purposes of his new functions introduced by the 1988 Act, namely the powers to apply for prohibition orders under section 25A of the 1982 Act and to apply for judicial review under section 25D of that Act (5.41A ff., below). Similar amendments were made in section 16(2) and 16(3) (4.123, 126 of main text).

4.112A Section 16 applies to health service bodies. Section 16(1A), inserted by Schedule 4 of the National Health Service and Community Care Act 1990 (para.6), provides that in the case of a recognised fund-holding practice section 16(1) relates to all the accounts and records of members of the practice whether or not related to the allotted sum.

Documents

4.119 The amendment noted at 4.112 above removes any doubt there might have been whether the auditor's powers were restricted by the words 'necessary for the purposes of the audit'.

4.120 See 4.112, above.

4.121 The District Audit Service and firms undertaking audits under the Local Government Finance Act 1982 have registered as data users under the Data Protection Act 1984 in respect of their statutory audits. This enables them to use software to create new data from existing personal data or to use their own computing facilities to hold personal data from manual records which have not been computerised – and therefore not registered – by the authority.

Information, explanation and facilities

4.123, 126, 127 For ' the purposes of the audit' read 'the purposes of the auditor's functions under the 1982 Act' (4.112, above).

Evidence on oath

4.130-1 In *Lloyd* v. *McMahon*, [1987] A.C. 625, Lord Keith, in considering whether a district auditor's decision vitiated by unfairness could be cured by appeal, said 'Evidence may be given on oath, which is not possible before the auditor' (p.697E). Lord Templeman, in the same context, said 'The auditor does not take evidence on oath' (p.715G), a statement of fact which is correct as a matter of general practice (as stated in para.4.131, main text) and in its application to the particular case. There is nothing in the law report, either in the speeches or in the report of the arguments of counsel, to indicate that consideration was given to section 16 of the Evidence Act 1851 and to the conflicting views thereon expressed in *R.* v. *Roberts*, as set out in the main text (para.4.130). The remarks quoted above do not appear as an essential, if as any, part of the reasoning leading to the conclusion that any unfairness by the auditor could be cured by appeal. That conclusion was itself *obiter*, since it was held that the auditor's procedure was fair. It thus appears questionable whether Lord Keith's *dictum* that the auditor cannot take evidence on oath should be regarded as authoritative.

In line 10 on page 110, for *'The County Court Practice,* 1984' read 'the current *County Court Practice'.*

Privilege, public interest and confidentiality

Self-incrimination

4.135,n.25   For '5th edn., p.281' of *Cross,* read '7th edn., p.426.' See also *Bank of England* v. *Riley, The Times,* 1 November 1990, where it was held that a person required to provide information and documents under the Banking Act 1987 (s.42) could not claim privilege against self-incrimination.

Legal professional privilege

4.139   For s.175, Companies Act 1948' read 's.452, Companies Act 1985'.

Public interest

4.143   Section 2 of the Official Secrets Act 1911 was replaced by the Official Secrets Act 1989, which restricts offences of unauthorised disclosure to official information relating to security and intelligence, defence, international relations, crime and special investigation powers.

Confidentiality

4.144A   Under legislation formerly applicable to health service audit, auditors appointed by the Secretary of State had access to documents of a health authority and power to require information for the purposes of the audit from members and officers of the authority (National Health Service (Audit of Accounts of Health Authorities) Regulations 1982, S.I. 1982/277). It was accepted practice under those provisions, upheld by the Department of Health's legal branch and Chief Medical Officer, that auditors had access to medical records of a health authority. This applies under the wider provisions of section 16 of the Local Government Finance Act 1982, which also extends the auditor's powers to include access to the documents and accounts of contractors, including family health service contractors (e.g. general practitioners and dentists) employed by health service bodies. Auditors are informed by the Audit Commission that they should respect the professional sensitivity of health authority staff when it is necessary to exercise these powers. See also 4.158, below.

Remedies

4.146,n.31   For '5th edn., pp.599-600' of *Cross*, read '7th edn., p.685'.

4.149,n.32   For 'pp.629 ff.' of *Wade*, read '(6th edn.), pp.649 ff'.

Bankers' records

4.150 For references to Companies Act 1948, sections 167 and 175(b), substitute references to Companies Act 1985, sections 434 and 452(1A),(1B).

Powers of the Audit Commission

4.154 Section 13(4) of the 1982 Act, as amended, does not apply to health service bodies (National Health Service and Community Care Act 1990, Sch.4, para.3).

Disclosure of information

4.157 In line 2, for 'the purposes of the audit' read 'the purposes of the auditor's functions under the 1982 Act' (4.112, above).

4.158 Section 30(1) of the 1982 Act was amended by Schedule 4 of the National Health Service and Community Care Act 1990 (para.2) to extend the permissible grounds for disclosure, in the case of a health service body, to disclosure for the purposes of the functions of the Secretary of State and the Comptroller and Auditor General under the National Health Service Act 1977.

The 1990 Code of Audit Practice requires auditors, in the exercise of professional care, to preserve where appropriate the confidentiality of sensitive information received during the audit (para.12(h)).

4.158A In *Bookbinder* v. *Tebbit*, 20 May 1991, unreported, Drake J. set aside subpoenas served by the plaintiff in a libel action to obtain evidence from audit staff who had enquired into expenditure relevant to the subject-matter of the alleged libel. He upheld submissions on behalf of the audit staff:

(1)   that public interest immunity applied, under established case law, where disclosure of information obtained by a body or person carrying out statutory investigations was likely to inhibit the obtaining of information for the purpose of such investigations; and that audit under the 1982 Act was such a case;

(2)   that audit evidence would involve breach of section 30(1), Local Government Finance Act 1982, since although the local authority concerned had consented to disclosure of the information sought, the information also related to the people who supplied it to the audit staff and those people had not consented;

(3)   that on the facts the plaintiff had not shown that audit evidence was necessary to dispose fairly of the case.

CHAPTER 5

SPECIAL JURISDICTION OF THE AUDITOR

I INTRODUCTION

Additional powers

5.6A   The Local Government Act 1988 conferred new powers on local government auditors enabling them to take early action to restrain an authority from unlawful action affecting the accounts. Auditors were empowered for this purpose to issue prohibition orders or to apply for judicial review. The new powers are considered in detail below as an additional section to this chapter (5.41A ff., below).

Health service bodies

5.6B   The National Health and Community Care Act 1990, in applying Part III of the Local Government Finance Act 1982 to some extent to the audit of health service bodies, specifically excluded sections 19, 20 and 25A to 25D (Sch.4, paras.9, 10, 16, 17). The 1990 Act did place some responsibility on the health service auditor in respect of unlawful conduct, however. Section 20(3) of that Act requires the auditor for the time being to refer forthwith to the Secretary of State any case where he has reason to believe that a body or officer has made or is about to make a decision involving the incurring of unlawful expenditure or has taken or is about to take a course of action which if pursued to its conclusion would be unlawful and likely to cause loss or deficiency. The wording is similar to that of paragraphs (a) and (b) of section 25A(1) of the 1982 Act relating to prohibition orders (5.41B, below) and the observations at 5.41D, below, may have some application.

5.6C   The 1990 Code of Audit Practice requires all auditors to keep under review the legality of authorities' transactions (para.34). On the other hand it states that there is no duty on the health service auditor to seek out matters for referral to the Secretary of State, but that he should consider matters relevant to section 20(3) arising at audit or raised by members, officers or others, and also any likelihood of expenditure exceeding resources (para.83). Auditors are not required by statute to consult with a body or its officers before referring a matter to the Secretary of State, but should give them the opportunity to respond so far as time permits, unless the circumstances make it inappropriate to do so (para.84).

III THE AUDITORS JURISDICTION – TIME

Commencing date

5.18A The first sentence of 5.18 in the main text applies also to the health service auditor who is thus also empowered to conduct a current audit. The auditor's duty under section 20(3) of the 1990 Act in respect of unlawfulness (5.6B, above) is attached to the auditor 'for the time being', so that even if an auditor's appointment were expressed to be limited to the end of the audit of a particular year's accounts he would be under a duty to refer to the Secretary of State any decision or course of action, actual or projected, in a subsequent year which fell within the terms of the subsection and which came to his notice before the completion of his audit.

The closed audit

5.29A In general it would appear that the rule of *functus officio* discussed in paragraphs 5.23-29 of the main text would apply to the health service auditor. However, the fact that the duty under section 20(3) of the 1990 Act in respect of unlawfulness is laid on the 'auditor for the time being' may be considered to imply that he should refer to the Secretary of State any decision or course of action within the terms of the section which comes to his notice even though it took place in a year for which the audit is closed.

IV   THE AUDITOR'S JURISDICTION – SUBJECT-MATTER

5.39   Similar considerations to those stated as formerly applying to the determination of values in valuation lists under Part V of the General Rate Act 1967 now apply to non-domestic rating lists under Part III of the Local Government Finance Act 1988.

V   LOCAL GOVERNMENT ACT 1988 – ADDITIONAL AUDIT POWERS

5.41A Section 30 of the Local Government Act 1988 and Schedule 4 thereto inserted new sections in Part III of the Local Government Finance Act 1982 giving auditors new powers to issue prohibition orders (ss.25A-25C) and to apply for judicial review (s.25D). In introducing the clauses in the House of Lords, the Earl of Caithness said:

> '... The provisions in the amendments derive from the [Widdicombe] Committee's recommendations that the Audit Service should be empowered to apply legal remedies more quickly to stop a local authority incurring unlawful expenditure or loss... The general effect of the amendments is to enable the appointed auditor of the authority to act directly to issue an order to prevent the authority from incurring unlawful expenditure or loss or from entering an unlawful item of account. Auditors will also be able to make an application to the courts for judicial review of a decision or failure to act by an authority which would have an effect on the accounts... I believe these amendments extend the scope of the existing audit legislation in an important and sensible way. Giving auditors the power to challenge unlawful action at an early stage, we can reduce the risk of authorities getting into difficulties as a result of spending illegally or incurring unlawful losses, and also reduce in the future the need for long and difficult surcharge cases...'

The powers of sections 25A to 25D do not apply to the audits of health service bodies (5.6B, above).

Prohibition orders

5.41B Section 25A(1) of the 1982 Act provides that the person who is for the time being the auditor in relation to the accounts of the body may issue a prohibition order if he has reason to believe that the body under audit or an officer of the body:

'(a) is about to make or has made a decision which involves or would involve the body incurring expenditure which is unlawful; or

(b) is about to take or has taken a course of action which, if pursued to its conclusion, would be unlawful and likely to cause a loss or deficiency; or

(c) is about to enter an item of account, the entry of which is unlawful'.

The subsection provides that the actions of a committee or sub-committee of the body or of any other person (not being an officer) authorised to act on behalf of the body shall be treated as the action of the body itself.

5.41C It seems that action could be take under paragraph (b) of section 25A(1) where a body decides, or appears to be about to decide, *not* to take action which it is required by law to take, and as a result a loss or deficiency is likely to be caused. An example could be a decision to cease making charges where there is a statutory duty to do so, as in *R. v. Roberts*, 1901 (main text, 7.7). However, some difficulty may be felt in fitting the language of section 25A to an order to enforce a negative (e.g., to desist from not making a charge). And it seems that the section could hardly apply to a case where the body simply failed to take action required by law as opposed to deciding that it would not take such action. But these situations could clearly be dealt with by the auditor's other new power to apply for judicial review (5.41Q, below).

5.41D The duty of the health service auditor to refer matters to the Secretary of State under section 20(3) of the National Health Service and Community Care Act 1990 (5.6B, above) arises in the same circumstances as those justifying a prohibition order under paragraphs (a) and (b) of section 25A(1) of the 1982 Act, and the questions mentioned above may possibly arise. The health service auditor cannot apply for judicial review, but in case of doubt whether section 20(3) is applicable he has an undoubted power to issue a report under section 15 of the 1982 Act, a copy of which would go to the Secretary of State under section 18(4) as amended.

5.41E An order in respect of an unlawful item of account under section 25A(1)(c) can be made only where it appears that a body or officer is about to enter such an item of account. It does not apply to an item which has already been entered, nor, apparently, to an entry which is not expected to be made until some time later (e.g., an entry in respect of accounting treatment decided at budget time which would not be effected until the accounts were in course of being closed after the end of the financial year). Again, both these situations could be dealt with by judicial review. The auditor may also attack under section 19, Local Government Finance Act 1982, an item already entered which he considers contrary to law.

Procedure

5.41F A prohibition order must be addressed to the body or officer concerned, specify the decision, course of action or item of account to which it relates and require the body or officer to desist from making or implementing the decision, taking the course of action or entering the item of account in question (s.25A(2)). Where a body has two or more auditors an order may be issued by one or both as they determine (s.25A(3)). A copy of the order must be served on the body or officer to whom it is addressed and, if addressed to an officer, on his employing body. A copy may also be served on such other persons as the auditor considers appropriate (s.25A(4)). This would enable the auditor, for example, to serve a copy of an order addressed to an authority on a person (other than an officer) whose action on behalf of the authority is treated as the action of the body under section 25A(1) (5.41B, above), or on a third party who may be considering entering into a contract of which the legality is questioned by the order.

5.41G The provisions relating to the effective date of the order are somewhat obscure. Subsection (2)(c) of section 25A provides that the order must state the date on which (subject to subsection (5)) it is to take effect, being a date not earlier than the date of service of a copy or copies of the order required by subsection (4). Subsection (5) states that an order shall not have effect unless, not later than seven days after the date of service mentioned in subsection (2)(c), the auditor serves on the body (and on an officer to whom an order is addressed) a statement of reasons for his belief as to the grounds for an order under subsection (1). It may be argued that since observance of the condition cannot be established until the statement of reasons is served the order can only then take effect, leaving open the possibility of a body or officer taking the action intended to be prohibited in any period between service of the order and the statement, even though the statement is served within seven days. But this interpretation would apparently mean that there would be no point in serving the order before the statement and therefore that the seven-day allowance would be nugatory. It seems that the more likely intention of Parliament was that the order would take effect immediately but would lapse after seven days if a statement had not by then been served, and that a construction to resolve the ambiguity in that sense would be preferable.

5.41H If an order is or becomes ineffective because the auditor fails to meet the seven-day deadline for his statement of reasons it appears that it would be open to him to issue a fresh order. Generally, the danger of a body seeking to avoid the effect of a prohibition order by entering into contractual commitments or other pre-emptive action before an order takes effect may in some cases be lessened by giving notice of intention to make the order to third parties with whom the body intends to deal, since they may be reluctant to contract until the law is clarified. Otherwise, recourse may be had, in appropriate cases, to the auditor's power to apply for judicial review.

5.41I A copy of an order or statement is to be served on an officer at the office at which he is employed (s.25A(6)). As to service on a local authority, and generally as to service by post, see main text, paragraph 4.95.

5.41J A prohibition order may at any time be revoked (but not varied) by the body's auditor for the time being (s.25A(7)). If an order needs revision, for example because of error or if the auditor agrees to representations to vary its scope, it would be necessary to revoke it and issue a fresh order, supported by a fresh statement of reasons.

Restriction on issue

5.41K The auditor may not issue a prohibition order in respect of any matter on which the chief finance officer has made a report to the council, with a copy to the auditor, in exercise of his powers under section 114 of the Local Government Finance Act 1988 (6.40A, below) during the period beginning with the issue of that report and ending with the day (if any) on which the body's consideration of the report under section 115(2) of the 1988 Act begins (s.25AA of the Local Government Finance Act 1982, inserted by s.137 and Sch.12, para.3(3) of the 1988 Act). The chief finance officer's report itself acts as an interim prohibition of the course of conduct to which it relates during the period for which the auditor's power to issue a prohibition order is restricted (s.115(5)-(7)/1988).

Effect of order

5.41L Subject to section 25A(5) (5.41G, above) and to any decision on appeal, a prohibition order has effect from the date stated in the order until it is revoked. So long as the order has effect it will not be lawful for the body concerned or any officer of that body to take any action against which the prohibition is directed (s.25B(1)). Thus any action in contravention of an order could result in action by the auditor under section 19 or 20 of the Local Government Finance Act 1982, or could be restrained by application for judicial review.

Appeals

5.41M Not later than 28 days after service of the statement of reasons for a prohibition order, the body, but not any officer, may appeal against the order to the High Court (s.25B(3)). No right of appeal is conferred on officers or third parties, whose only possible means of challenge of the order would be by application for judicial review on the ground that the auditor had exercised his discretion in breach of the principles of administrative law (5.41U, below).

5.41N Section 25B(4) provides that the High Court may order the payment by the body of expenses incurred by the auditor in connection with an appeal. The wording, in referring to expenses rather than costs, follows corresponding provisions in the Local Government Finance Act 1982 (see main text, 9.42 ff.). Section 25B(5) goes further in providing that any expenses reasonably incurred by the auditor in or in connection with the issue of a prohibition order shall be recoverable by him from the body concerned. Section 25C(2) exempts the auditor from any action in respect of loss or damage alleged to be caused by a prohibition order issued in good faith, but reserves the right of the court to award costs against the auditor on an appeal under section 25B(3).

Contracts

5.41P In respect of a contract to dispose of or acquire an interest in land made by a body before a prohibition order is issued, but rendered unlawful to complete because of the order, the other party's remedy in damages is not prejudiced (s.25C(2)). No such provision in respect of other contracts is included in the Act.

Judicial review

5.41Q Section 25D of the Local Government Finance Act 1982, inserted by section 30 and Schedule 4 of the Local Government Act 1988, empowers the auditor appointed in relation to the accounts of a body to apply for judicial review with respect to any decision of the body, or any failure by the body to act, which in either case it is reasonable to believe would have an effect on the accounts of the body. The court may order payment of the auditor's expenses as for appeals against prohibition orders (5.41N, above). No time is specified in which the effect on the accounts may arise, so it is not limited to effects arising within the current financial year. It is not necessary for the effect on the accounts to be an adverse effect or involve expenditure. An income-raising scheme beyond the body's powers and an unlawful decision or failure to act as required by law in respect of transfers between accounts would also be susceptible to challenge by application for judicial review.

5.41R For the remedies available within the scope of judicial review, and the relevant procedure, see main text, 8.49-51. In appropriate cases, interim relief can be obtained from the court at the same time as leave to commence proceedings or subsequently. This might take the form of a stay, prohibiting the body under audit from taking or implementing a decision which is challenged pending the ruling of the court in the substantive cases (R.S.C. O.53, r.3(10)); *R.* v. *Secretary of State for Education and Science, ex parte Avon C.C.,* [1991] 1 Q.B. 558 (C.A.).

5.41S In general any decision or course of action which could be stopped by a prohibition order could also be challenged by application for judicial review. On such an application the court could stop any unlawful action by injunction or order of prohibition and could quash any unlawful decision or unlawful item of account by order of certiorari.

It could also correct, by order of mandamus, any failure to take action required by law, whether or not involving a specific decision not to take such action. Simply by declaration it could resolve disputed questions of law and hence in most cases ensure correction of any unlawfulness, or in other cases open the way to enforcement by the auditor under section 19 or 20 of the Local Government Finance Act 1982.

5.41T An application by a district auditor for judicial review under section 25D was upheld in *R.* v. *Wirral M.B.C., ex parte Milstead* (1989), 87 L.G.R. 611, the court making an order of certiorari to quash as unlawful a decision to enter into a factoring agreement to sell its anticipated receipts from future sales of land and an order of prohibition to restrain the council from further steps to factor receipts. For further details see 6.22A, below.

Matters common to additional powers

5.41U Both the issue of prohibition orders and applications for judicial review are powers, not duties. The auditor has a discretion whether or not to exercise the powers, a discretion which he must exercise in accordance with the normal principles of administrative law. So he must act fairly in his procedure, must take into account all relevant considerations and exclude irrelevant considerations. If he fails in any of these matters, or reaches a decision which no reasonable auditor could reach, his decision could apparently itself be the subject of judicial review on the application of officers or third parties affected by his decision, or could be attacked on this basis in response to his own application for judicial review.

5.41V The Local Government Act 1988, which conferred the additional powers on the auditor, also, by section 30(2), amended section 16 of the Local Government Finance Act 1982, extending the auditor's powers to obtain documents, information and explanations, originally applicable 'for the purposes of the audit', so that they now extend to such items as he thinks necessary 'for the purposes of his functions under this Act', which includes the new functions inserted in the 1982 Act by the 1988 Act.

5.41W It is to be noted that there is a difference in phraseology relating to the auditor between sections 25A and 25D of the 1982 Act. Section 25A confers the power to issue prohibition orders on 'the person who is for the time being the auditor in relation to the accounts' of the body. Section 25D gives the power to apply for judicial review to 'the auditor appointed in relation to the accounts' of the body. The reason for the different wording is not clear. It may be considered that the phrase 'for the time being' is used in section 25A so that even if an auditor's appointment were expressed to be limited to the end of the audit of a particular year's accounts he would be empowered to issue a prohibition order in respect of matters arising during a subsequent year which came to his notice before his audit was completed; and that it was not intended that this should apply in the case of judicial review. But no reason is apparent why such a distinction should be drawn. Nor is it clear that the wording in section 25D would preclude the auditor in those circumstances from action under the section; until his last year's audit is complete he is still an 'auditor appointed in relation to the accounts' of the body. If there were an intention to restrict him to action in respect of events in the year he was auditing it could easily have been clearly expressed. There may have been another reason, not readily apparent, for the difference in wording, but it seems possible that it may be a variation not having any effect of substance.

Code of Audit Practice

5.41X The 1990 Code of Audit Practice includes the following provisions and comments in respect of the powers under sections 25A and 25D of the 1982 Act. The powers should be used only where the matter is significant either in amount or principle or both (para.78). There is no duty on the auditor to seek out matters calling for the exercise of the powers, and local government electors have no rights in respect of the powers corresponding to the rights of question and objection under section 17 of the 1982 Act. But the auditor should give consideration to any such matters arising at audit, including matters raised by members and officers of the body or members of the public, and should give particular consideration to any report of a chief finance officer or monitoring officer (6.40A-D, below) as to the possibility of unlawful expenditure or items of account, of unlawful action leading to loss or deficiency, or of expenditure exceeding resources (para.79). There is no duty on the auditor to consult with the body before exercising these powers, but he should do so as far as consistent with the prompt exercise of the powers in the public interest (para.80).

CHAPTER 6

ILLEGALITY

I ITEMS OF ACCOUNT CONTRARY TO LAW – *ULTRA VIRES*

Items of account contrary to law

6.1 Section 19 of the Local Government Finance Act 1982, as amended, does not apply to the audit of health service bodies (National Health Service and Community Care Act 1990, Sch.4 para.9). But see 5.6B-C, above, as to responsibility of the health service auditor in respect of unlawful decisions involving the possibility of unlawful expenditure, or of loss or deficiency. Paragraph 34 of the 1990 Code of Audit Practice requires all auditors to keep under review the legality of authorities' transactions.

6.2 The decision in *Wilkinson* v. *Doncaster M.B.C.* was upheld by the Court of Appeal, (1985) 84 L.G.R. 257.

Ultra vires

6.5,n.3 Section 9 of the European Communities Act 1972 has been replaced by sections 35 to 35B of the Companies Act 1985 as amended and inserted by section 108, Companies Act 1989, which provide more comprehensive protection against possible unfair results of the *ultra vires* doctrine in respect of companies.

Application to local authorities etc.

6.6 In *Hazell* v. *Hammersmith and Fulham L.B.C.*, [1991] 2 W.L.R. 372, 392, the question arose of the applicability of the doctrine of *ultra vires* to a London borough. Section 1(2) of the London Government Act 1963 provides that if Her Majesty thinks fit to grant a charter of incorporation to the inhabitants of a London borough the charter may make provision with respect to the name of the borough and other specified matters. It was accordingly argued that a London borough is a corporation created by royal charter, and as such, by well-established case law, has at common law the full capacity of a natural person. The House of Lords, rejecting this argument, held that where a statute authorises the grant of a royal charter the powers of a corporation created by such a charter depend on the true construction and intent of the statute; and on that basis a charter made pursuant to the Act of 1963 did not confer on the borough or the council any greater power than the statutory powers exercisable by other London boroughs (which could also be created by ministerial order under section 1(3)).

Varying use of the term

6.7 It has now been held by the Court of Appeal that in company law the term *ultra vires* should strictly be confined to acts beyond the objects of the company and that transactions within those objects may vest rights in third parties even if carried out in excess or abuse of powers. (*Rolled Steel Products (Holdings) Ltd.* v. *British Steel Corporation*, [1986] Ch.246, 303G). As to possible application of this decision to local authorities, see 6.110, below.

6.7,n.5   For 'pp.39-43, 348-9' of *Wade*, read '(6th edn.), pp.41-4 ,389-91'.

6.7,n.6   For 'pp.40-1, 415' of *Wade*, read '(6th edn.), pp.41-2, 467'.

6.8,n.7   For reference to *Halsbury*, read '4th edn. (Reissue), Vol.7(1), para.945'.

Mandatory and directory requirements

6.9   In *R.* v. *Lambeth L.B.C., ex parte Sharp*, [1987] J.P.L. 440, a Court of Appeal decision, Woolf L.J. said that it was almost invariably unhelpful to consider what were the consequences of non-compliance with statutory conditions by classifying them as containing mandatory or directory provisions; it had to be asked what was the particular provision designed to achieve, and non-compliance had to be considered in the context of the particular circumstances of the case. The *Lambeth* case concerned a failure by the council to follow statutory procedure in giving public notice of a proposal to give itself deemed planning permission. The court held that the applicant himself had not been prejudiced by the failure but that he was making the application on behalf of the public and that the planning permission should be quashed as in breach of a requirement fundamental to the operation of this particular planning procedure.

Incidental powers

6.22A In *R.* v. *Wirral M.B.C., ex parte Milstead* (1989), 87 L.G.R. 611, the Divisional Court granted an application by the district auditor for judicial review and for an order of certiorari to quash, as unlawful, decisions of the council to 'factor' future anticipated receipts from sales of council houses and other property, and an order of prohibition to restrain them from taking any further steps to factor such receipts. The effect of a factoring agreement would have been to sell, for a current payment, the right to receipts from future sales of land, and the benefit which the council expected to get from the agreement was that the sums received would be counted as sums received in respect of disposals of land in the current year, which would increase the limit of prescribed capital expenditure which the council would be permitted to incur under the provisions of Part VIII of the Local Government, Planning and Land Act 1980.

6.22B The council argued that the factoring agreement was lawful under section 111(1) of the Local Government Act 1972 as incidental to the discharge of their functions, which included the exercise of the power to sell land. But the court held that the factoring agreement was not incidental to the selling of land since it was concerned with the disposal of the proceeds of sale, which cannot be said to be incidental to the sale of the land. The agreement was therefore not authorised by section 111(1) of the 1972 Act and was beyond the powers of the council. Also, the factoring receipts would not be 'sums received in respect of disposal of land' under the 1980 Act; they would be sums received in respect of sums payable at a later date out of the proceeds of land. They would therefore not have had the desired result of increasing the limit of prescribed capital expenditure under the 1980 Act, would consequently have served no useful purpose and would be held unlawful as being irrational or based on wrong legal advice.

6.22C In *Hazell* v. *Hammersmith and Fulham L.B.C.*, [1991] 2 W.L.R. 372, the House of Lords held that methods of interest rate risk management such as interest rate swaps (under which parties contracted to pay or receive the difference over a period between interest payable on specified sums at fixed or variable rates of interest) were not covered by section 111 of the Local Government Act 1972 as 'calculated to facilitate or conducive or incidental' to the function of borrowing, and hence were not capable of being within the powers of local authorities.

6.22D The council had entered into very extensive swaps and similar transactions with banks, to a far greater extent than could be justified as debt management. The object was to make a profit by trading in the capital market, but the trend of interest rates had been such that if the transactions were enforceable they would result in a loss in excess of £100 million. Following audit representations the council limited its transactions to an 'interim strategy' to reduce the extent of its exposure to loss, and later, having itself received legal advice that the transactions were unlawful, ceased to make payments due to the banks.

6.22E The auditor applied to the court under section 19 of the Local Government Finance Act 1982 for a declaration that the relevant items of account were contrary to law and an order for rectification of the accounts. The council did not propose to dispute the application but a number of banks sought and were allowed to be joined in the proceedings. The Divisional Court granted the auditor's application, holding that no such swaps or the like were capable of being within the powers of local authorities. On appeal by the banks, the Court of Appeal held that a swap entered into with reference to a particular debt could be lawful under section 111 of the 1972 Act as interest rate risk management incidental to the function of borrowing, but that authorities were not empowered to trade with a view to profit. On the facts they held that the transactions before the interim strategy period were unlawful as tainted with the improper purpose of trading, but that the transactions during the interim strategy period were lawful. The auditor appealed to the House of Lords.

6.22F The House of Lords, upholding the appeal, reinstated the original orders of the Divisional Court declaring all the relevant items of account contrary to law, including those of the interim strategy period, and ordering rectification of the accounts with liberty to the parties to apply to the court in the absence of agreement. In particular it was held:

(1)   that since section 111 is expressly made 'subject to the provisions of this Act', regard must be had to Schedule 13 to the Act, which contained extremely detailed provisions providing a code which defined and consequently limited the powers of a local authority with regard to borrowing, thereby precluding swap activities being treated as incidental to the borrowing function;

(2)   that swap transactions did not facilitate the original function of borrowing - they were a separate and distinct speculative activity aimed at reducing the burden of interest on money already borrowed;

(3)   that legislation relating to building societies, under which powers to enter into swap transactions were at first limited and then extended, illustrates that it is for Parliament and not for the courts to balance the risks and advantages of such powers and decide whether to proceed, if at all, by stages;

(4)   that the interim strategy activities were not incidental to the original borrowing but to the initial *ultra vires* activities of unlawful interest rate swapping and accordingly suffered from the same stigma of being unlawful.

6.22G Following the House of Lords decision, the Audit Commission received legal advice to the effect that all interest rate swap and similar contracts entered into by local authorities were *ultra vires* and void and that money paid by or to a local authority under such void contracts was recoverable by the person who paid it, but that if entitlement to, or the extent of, restitution was disputed an authority had power to enter into a *bona fide* compromise, in the reasonable exercise of discretion, in order to settle a claim made by or against the authority.

Finality of decisions

6.25,n.26 For 'pp.225-8, 249 ff.' of *Wade* read '(6th edn.), pp. 253-7, 279 ff.'.

Miscellaneous items of account

Loans fund advances

6.32A In *Stockdale* v. *Haringey L.B.C.*, [1989] R.A. 107, the Court of Appeal upheld the Divisional Court's decision in granting the district auditor a declaration that advances from the council's loans fund in excess of borrowing powers were contrary to law, and an order for rectification of accounts. The council contended that the readvancing of moneys repaid by spending accounts did not constitute statutory borrowing, but the courts held that the only provision authorising the use of loans fund money for another purpose (other than redemption and repayment of debt) was paragraph 19 of Schedule 13 to the Local Government Act 1972, which by virtue of paragraph 19(4) was subject to the statutory controls on borrowing. (The provisions of Schedule 13 relating to loans pools were repealed by the Local Government and Housing Act 1989. Part IV of that Act introduced a new regime for the control of local authority capital finance, under which an authority's borrowing may not exceed an aggregate credit limit related to the issue of ministerial credit approvals, and capital expenditure which is not covered by credit approval or otherwise excepted must be charged to revenue (ss.41-44)).

Compliance with accountancy principles: income and expenditure basis

6.36   It does not appear that the conclusions in this paragraph are affected by the changes made by Part VI of the Local Government Finance Act 1988 in substituting general funds for general rate funds, or by the changes in housing legislation noted at 3.15, above.

6.36-9 For statutory provisions concerning accounts of income and expenditure, and proper practices relating thereto, see 3.2C-D and 4.50A, above.

6.38   The comments in the last two sentences appear equally applicable to the community charge regime; authorities are required to raise by community charge or precept the total estimated expenditure to be incurred during the year which is to be met from community charges (Local Government Finance Act 1988, ss.32, 68).

6.39   In the last sentence for the references to Housing Acts substitute reference to the Local Government and Housing Act 1989, sections 75 to 78 and Schedule 4.

6.40   The case here referred to as *Stirling D.C. Stated Case* is now reported as *Commission for L.A. Accounts in Scotland* v. *Stirling D.C.*, 1984 S.L.T. 442.

Officers' reports on illegality

6.40A The Local Government Finance Act 1988, section 114, placed new responsibilities in the field of illegality upon the officer responsible for financial administration under section 151 of the Local Government Act 1972, who is referred to in the 1988 Act as the chief finance officer of the authority. He must make a report under the section if it appears to him that the authority or a committee or officer of the authority has made or is about to make a decision involving the incurrence of unlawful expenditure, or has taken or is about to take a course of action which, if pursued to its conclusion, would be unlawful and likely to cause a loss or deficiency, or is about to enter an unlawful item of account (subs.(2)). He must also report if it appears to him that the authority will incur expenditure in a financial year in excess of its available resources, including sums borrowed (subs.(3)).

6.40B The duties of a chief finance officer under this section must be performed by him personally, or if he is unable to act through absence or illness, by a member of his staff nominated by him for the purpose, who must be a member of specified accountancy bodies unless there is no such member on his staff (subss.(5),(6)). The authority must provide him with such staff, accommodation and other resources as are in his opinion sufficient to allow his duties under the section to be performed (subs.(7)). In preparing a report under the section he must consult so far as practicable with the head of paid service and the monitoring officer appointed under sections 4 and 5 of the Local Government and Housing Act 1989 (subs.(3A)/1988, inserted by the 1989 Act, Sch.5).

6.40C Copies of the report must be sent to each member of the authority and to the auditor (s.114(4)/1988). The authority itself must consider the report within 21 days and must then decide whether it agrees or disagrees with the views contained in the report and what action (if any) it proposes to take in consequence of it. The authority is prohibited, until consideration of the report is concluded, from pursuing the course under report or, where the report relates to expenditure in excess of resources, from making new agreements involving expenditure. Expenditure resulting from non-compliance with these prohibitions will be *ultra vires* (s.115). The auditor must be informed as soon as practicable of the date, time and place of a meeting under section 115, and of any decision made at the meeting (s.116). As to the restriction on the auditor's power to issue a prohibition order during the period of consideration under section 115, see 5.41K, above.

6.40D The Local Government and Housing Act 1989, section 5, requires local authorities to designate one of their officers as monitoring officer and to provide him with staff, accommodation and other resources sufficient in his opinion for his duties. He may be the head of paid service but may not be the chief finance officer (subs.(1)). His duty is to report to the authority on any proposal, decision or omission which appears to him likely to result in contravention of any enactment, rule of law or statutory code of practice or to give rise to maladministration or injustice as mentioned in Part III of the Local Government Act 1974 (subs.(2)). He must consult with the head of paid service and the chief finance officer in preparing the report, and must send a copy to each member of the authority (subs.(3)). His duties must be performed personally or in his absence or illness by a nominated deputy (subs.(7)). The authority must itself consider the report within 21 days, and ensure that implementation of any relevant proposals or decisions is suspended until a day after consideration is concluded (subss.(5), (6)). The section does not require copies of the report to be sent to auditors; nor is there any provision corresponding to that restricting the auditor's power to issue a prohibition order during the period of consideration of a chief finance officer's report (5.41K, above).

6.40E Generally on responsibilities of officers, see also main text, 6.172 ff.

Companies under local authority control/influence

6.40F Section 70 of the Local Government and Housing Act 1989 empowers the Secretary of State to make provision by order regulating, forbidding or requiring the taking of specified actions by companies which by virtue of sections 68 and 69 of the Act are defined as under the control of, or subject to the influence of, a local authority (subs.(1)). The order may require a company or local authority to obtain the consent of the Secretary of State or of the Audit Commission before taking any action or course of action (subs. (5)). For companies under their control, local authorities are required to ensure, as far as practicable, that they comply with the provisions of any such order. If a local authority fails in that duty, any payment it makes to the company, and any other expenditure incurred by the authority in contravention of any such provision, will be deemed for the purposes of Part III of the Local Government Finance Act 1982 to be unlawful (subs.(2)).

6.40G For companies subject to the influence of a local authority an order under section 70 may prescribe requirements to be complied with by the authority as to conditions to be included in leases, licences, contracts, gifts, grants or loans made with or to a company (subs.(3)). If the authority fails to comply with the requirements of such an order any expenditure it incurs under the lease, etc., will be deemed to be unlawful for the purposes of Part III of the 1982 Act (subs.(4)).

II 'UNREASONABLENESS' – UNLAWFUL EXERCISE OF DISCRETION

Criteria for intervention

6.44   The cases referred to in this paragraph were followed in *Hemsted* v. *Lees* (1986), 18 H.L.R. 424, where an appeal by an objector against an auditor's decision was dismissed. The objector claimed that the rate fund contribution to the Housing Revenue Account was unlawful, mainly on the ground that the council had failed to consider market rental values. It was held that the authority were not obliged to relate its rents to market rents and that having regard to the minutes and the auditor's comparisons with other authorities, there was nothing to indicate that the local authority were not holding the scales fairly between tenants and ratepayers.

6.52   As to the conditions to be satisfied before an auditor could seek a declaration of illegality under section 19 of the 1982 Act in respect of allegedly wasteful expenditure which he may have previously reported as such, see 4.77A, above.

Other cases on judicial review of discretionary powers

6.54   In last line, for 'pp.362-5' of *Wade*, read '(6th edn.), pp.389-90, 407-10'.

The *Wednesbury* criteria to establish excess or abuse of discretion were the subject of comment by Lord Diplock in *Council of Civil Service Unions* v. *Minister for the Civil Service*, [1985] A.C. 374, 410 (the 'GCHQ case'), in the course of an analysis of the grounds for judicial review under the heads of 'illegality', 'irrationality' and 'procedural impropriety'. By 'irrationality', he said, he meant 'What can by now be succinctly referred to as "*Wednesbury* unreasonableness". It applies to a decision which is so outrageous in its defiance of logic or of accepted moral standards that no sensible person who had applied his mind to the question to be decided could have arrived at it'. In equating 'irrationality' with '*Wednesbury* 'unreasonableness', Lord Diplock appears to have been referring only to the third head of 'unreasonableness' in the *Wednesbury* judgment (6.43, main text). However, as pointed out by Lord Roskill at p.415, the GCHQ case was not concerned with *Wednesbury* principles and it does not appear that Lord Diplock's speech can be taken as excluding the other *Wednesbury* grounds of review for unreasonableness (taking account of irrelevant matters or failure to take account of relevant matters). The speech was later described by Lord Scarman as 'a valuable, and already classical, but certainly not exhaustive analysis' (*R.* v. *Secretary of State for the Environment, ex parte Notts. C.C.,* [1986] A.C. 240, 249). The use of 'irrationality' instead of 'unreasonableness in the *Wednesbury* sense' has been criticised in *Wade* (6th edn., pp.398-9), and by Lord Donaldson M.R. in *R.* v. *Devon C.C., ex parte G,* [1989] A.C. 573, 577F. But it has been widely used in judgments.

6.54,n.37 For 'pp.348-9, 391' of *Wade,* read '(6th edn.), pp.389-90, 442-3'.

6.57,n.41 For 'p.752' of *Wade,* read '(6th edn.), p.868'.

6.60,n.43 For 'pp.249 ff.' of *Wade,* read '(6th edn.), pp.279 ff.'

6.61,n.44 For 'pp.42, 263-7', of *Wade,* read '(6th edn.), pp.43, 293-303'.

6.61,n.45 For 'pp.349, 370' of *Wade,* read '(6th edn.), pp.390, 411'.

6.63   In line 4, for 'section 111 of the Housing Act 1957', read 'section 24 of the Housing Act 1985'.

6.64,n.48 For 'pp.319-346' of *Wade,* read '(6th edn.), pp.357-387'.

6.70   As to *Stirling D.C. Stated Case,* see 6.40, above.

6.70,n.51 Add '*Hemsted* v. *Lees* (1986), 18 H.L.R. 424' (6.44, above).

Unreasonableness beyond reason

6.82   Professor de Smith's criticism of Lord Greene's 'something overwhelming' test, referred to in this paragraph (n.54), was specifically considered by the Court of Appeal in the unreported case of *Sand & Gravel Association Ltd.* v. *Buckinghamshire C.C.,* CO/540/82, 14 November 1984. At first instance McNeill J. had referred with approval to de Smith's views, but they were firmly rejected by the Court of Appeal. After consideration of the cases cited by de Smith and by McNeill J., Purchase L.J. said:

> 'If the learned judge was drawing from these speeches any support for his contention that there had been some retreat from "overwhelming" as a description of the sort of evidence required, or that in some other way there had been a degree of mitigation of the test in the *Wednesbury* case, with respect to him I could not agree with that proposition'. (Transcript, Association of Official Shorthandwriters Ltd., p.33F.)

Mixed motives

6.90,n.60 For 'pp.388-390' of *Wade,* read '(6th edn.), pp.439-442'. See also *R.* v. *Ealing L.B.C., ex parte Times Newspapers Ltd.* (1986), 85 L.G.R. 316.

Unreasonableness and *ultra vires*

6.110 In *Rolled Steel Products (Holdings) Ltd.* v. *British Steel Corporation,* [1986] Ch. 246, the Court of Appeal held that in company law the term *ultra vires* should strictly be confined to describe the acts which are beyond the corporate capacity of a company as being altogether outside its objects, and should not be applied to transactions within the objects of a company but carried out in excess or abuse of the company's powers. Such a transaction, it was held, would be effective to vest rights in third parties (pp.302-3). In *Hazell* v. *Hammersmith and Fulham L.B.C.* (6.22C, above) it was argued by the banks before the Divisional Court that the *Rolled Steel* decision should be applied by analogy to statutory bodies, the statute under which they are created being treated as the equivalent of the memorandum which sets out the objects of a company. In support of that argument it was submitted that the law in relation to *ultra vires,* both in respect of public bodies and companies, has a common source in the decision of the House of Lords in *Ashbury Railway*

Carriage Co. Ltd. v. *Riche* (1875), L.R. 7 H.L. 653, and that the views expressed by Lord Sumner in *Roberts* v. *Hopwood*, [1925] A.C. 578, 602 (as quoted in main text, 6.109) were consistent with the argument. If the *Rolled Steel* decision were applicable to local authorities it would mean that if transactions entered into by an authority were capable of being lawful as within statutory powers, but were only unlawful because carried out for an inadmissible purpose or otherwise in abuse of powers, the contracts would not be void and would be enforceable against the authority by an innocent contracting party. The Divisional Court recognised the force of the argument, but expressed no conclusion upon it since it did not affect the question before the court whether items of account were contrary to law, but rather the consequences between the council and other parties in cases where the transactions are capable of being lawful, but are not lawful for other reasons ([1990] 2 Q.B. 697, 736 ff.). That question was not discussed by the Court of Appeal or the House of Lords.

III DUE AUTHORISATION

Delegation and agency

6.115,n.68 For 'pp.319-20' of *Wade*, read '(6th edn.), pp.357-8'.

6.115,n.69 Other cases in which action taken by junior officers has been held valid although functions have not been expressly delegated to them are *Cheshire C.C.* v. *Secretary of State for the Environment*, [1988] J.P.L. 30, in which power had been delegated to the Council Solicitor and the effective decision was taken by a member of his staff, and *R.* v. *Southwark L.B.C.*, *ex parte Bannerman*, [1990] 2 Admin. L.R. 634, in which the council's delegation scheme provided that where authority to take decisions was given to a chief officer the decision should be taken 'in the name of (but not necessarily personally by) such officer', and proceedings instituted on the recommendation of an officer of the Borough Valuer's Department acting in the Valuer's name were held valid.

6.116-8 In *R.* v. *Secretary of State for the Environment, ex parte Hillingdon L.B.C,* [1986] 1 W.L.R. 192, affirmed [1986] 1 W.L.R. 807, delegation to a single member was held invalid. It was held that the word 'committee' in section 101 of the Local Government Act 1972 had to be taken in the modern sense of the word as signifying a number of persons meeting together, and that this was confirmed by the language of Schedule 12 to the 1972 Act in referring to majorities, casting votes etc. In *Fraser* v. *Secretary of State for the Environment* (1987), 56 P.& C.R. 386, a standing order providing for action by an officer with the written approval of a chairman was held lawful on the basis that the officer had formed his opinion before seeking approval and it was the officer alone who had taken the action. But in *R.* v. *Port Talbot B.C.*, *ex parte Jones*, [1988] 2 All E.R. 207, the grant of a tenancy to a councillor under a similar arrangement was quashed where the officer deposed that had it not been for pressure by the chairman he would not have granted the tenancy.

6.118 For 'p.324' of *Wade*, read '(6th edn.), p.363'

Ratification

6.125,nn.78,79 For 'pp.323-4' of *Wade*, read '(6th edn.), pp.362-3'. In *Webb* v. *Ipswich B.C.* (1989), 21 H.L.R. 325, the Court of Appeal refused to allow ratification because an individual's legal rights had already been affected by the invalid act of an officer. *Warwick R.D.C.* v. *Miller-Mead* was distinguished because in that case the ratification was made before any effective step had been made to affect an individual's rights.

IV SUNDRY DECISIONS ON LEGALITY

Pay and emoluments of employees

Superannuation allowances

6.131 Minor amendments to this paragraph arise from amendment of the Representation of the People Act 1983 by the like Act of 1985 (s.24, Sch.4). Section 52(4) of the 1983 Act as originally enacted covered officers assigned by the council to assist in duties relating to registration and parliamentary elections. The provision in respect of elections now appears in section 28(5) of the 1983 Act as amended. Section 52(2) of the 1983 Act as amended requires approval of persons appointed as deputy registration officers by the council rather than by the Secretary of State. It does not appear that these amendments affect the position as to superannuation.

6.131,n.86 The name of the European Assembly has been changed to the European Parliament, and existing instruments amended to reflect the change (European Communities Act (Amendment) Act 1986, s.3).

Section 137, Local Government Act 1972 (formerly 'The Free Twopence')

6.144 Section 137 of the Local Government Act 1972 was substantially amended by the Local Government and Housing Act 1989 (s.36, Sch.2). The rate limit on expenditure was replaced by limits based on population. Expenditure must not only be in the interests of the area or its inhabitants, but must bring direct benefit to them and be proportionate to the benefit. Expenditure on economic development is the subject of specific statutory powers in sections 33-35 of the 1989 Act and section 137 is therefore no longer available for that purpose.

Administrative expenses

6.145-6 The matter mentioned in these paragraphs came before the courts in *Leicester City Council* v. *District Auditor for Leicester* (1985), 25 R.V.R. 191(Q.B.D.), 29 R.V.R. 162(C.A.). The council applied for judicial review of the auditor's report referred to in paragraph 6.146 and asked for declarations that expenditure on pay and related expenses concerned with section 137 projects was not incurred under section 137 and should not be charged to the section 137 account. The council relied mainly on a submission that staff are appointed under section 112 of the Local Government Act 1972, so that their pay is incurred under that section and not under section 137. The application was dismissed in the High Court and the Court of Appeal, the courts holding that since section 112 authorises the appointment of officers for discharge of the authority's functions, it only comes into effect when some other statute creates a function, in this case section 137, and the officers' pay and overheads are section 137 expenditure if incurred because they were engaged on a section 137 function.

Trust to carry forward unexpended balance invalid

6.146A *R. v. District Auditor No.3 Audit District, ex parte West Yorkshire Metropolitan C.C.* (1985), 26 R.V.R. 24, related to a council which was to be abolished from 1 April 1986 and would not be able to incur expenditure under section 137 in 1985/6 without the consent of the Secretary of State (Local Government (Interim Provisions) Act 1984, s.7(1)). The council therefore resolved to create a trust, funded by the unexpended balance of the 'free twopence' for 1984/5, and to authorise the trustees to apply the trust for the benefit of the inhabitants of the county in specified ways. The district auditor reported to the council that in his view the payment to the trustees would probably not be authorised by section 137 or by any other statutory provision. The council applied for judicial review of the auditor's report, seeking a declaration that the payment to the trustees would be within its powers. But the court held that the trust would be invalid since it could not take effect either as a charitable trust, because some of its purposes were non-charitable, or as a private trust, because the class of possible beneficiaries was too wide.

6.146B In both the *Leicester* and the *West Yorkshire* cases the courts expressed reservations whether judicial review was an appropriate remedy, since in each case the auditor had made no determination, the views expressed in his report being only provisional. But in each case the parties agreed that the matter should be decided quickly and the court agreed to hear the case because no other method was then available to achieve this. (It would now be possible for the auditor to initiate judicial review proceedings – 5.41Q, above).

V POWERS OF AUDITOR AND THE COURT

Declaration by the court

6.158 The Divisional Court judgment in *Hazell v. Hammersmith and Fulham L.B.C.*, [1990] 2 Q.B. 697, 735, (6.22C, above) records that it was accepted by all parties, rightly in the view of the court, that the court had a discretion whether or not to make a declaration. The banks argued that in any event the court, as a matter of discretion, should decline to grant a declaration, since this would permit the banks, in other proceedings, to contend that the transactions were valid until declared void. The court considered that this concern was misplaced, not only because the declaration would not normally bind third parties, but also because the declaration relates to the items of account and not to any transactions to which the items of account may relate.

The judgment went on to point out that in the reverse situation, where the lawfulness of a transaction had been established by a decision of a competent court, that may be decisive as to the lawfulness of an item of account; this was illustrated by the Irish audit case of *R. (Duckett) v. Calvert*, [1898] 2 I.R. 511, where two contracts for lighting a town, one by gas and one by electricity, had been recognised as valid by decrees of the county court on claims under the contracts. The auditor disallowed payments to the electricity company as unfounded and illegal since one lighting system was sufficient for the town, but it was held on appeal that it was not open to him to disallow payments under a contract recognised as valid by a competent court.

These matters were not referred to in the judgments of the higher courts in the *Hazell* case.

6.158,n.93 For 'p.523' of *Wade,* read '(6th edn.), pp.594-5'.

Order for repayment

Responsibility for authorising

6.163 On the question whether unlawful exercise or abuse of discretion is to be equated with *ultra vires*, and the effect on third parties, see 6.110, above.

6.163,n.99 For 'p.39' of *Wade*, read '(6th edn.), p.41'.

Responsibility of officers

6.172 For another aspect of the responsibility of officers, see 6.40A, above (Officers' reports on illegality).

6.176,n.108 For '15th edn., 104-5' of Clerk and Lindsell, *Torts*, read '16th edn., paras. 1-183, 1-184'.

Enforcement

6.183 Section 30 of the Bankruptcy Act 1914 was repealed by the Insolvency Act 1985 and was not re-enacted. Under section 382(2) of the Insolvency Act 1986, where the cause of action accrues before the commencement of the bankruptcy, an unliquidated claim in tort becomes a bankruptcy debt, since the bankrupt is deemed to become subject to that liability by reason of an obligation incurred at the time when the cause of action accrued (Halsbury, *Laws of England*, 4th edn., Reissue, Vol.3(2), 479-80).

Section 39 of the 1914 Act was replaced to the same effect, subject to modifications and additions, by sections 334-5, Insolvency Act 1986.

6.184(1) Enforcement of county court judgments or orders by execution against goods must be effected in the High Court if for £5000 or more, and may be if for £2000 or more (High Court and County Courts Jurisdiction Order 1991, S.I. 724, art.8).

6.184(8) Section 13 of the Courts and Legal Services Act 1990 provides for the making of administration orders irrespective of the amount owed (not yet in force).

6.184(9) For the statutory references, read 'ss.267-8, Insolvency Act 1986'.

6.184,n.117 Delete 'Sch.3, para.22'; add 'County Courts Act 1984,s.108'.

6.185 The law relating to bankruptcy is now for the most part contained in the Insolvency Act 1986 and in the Insolvency Rules 1986 (S.I. 1986/1925) and other rules made under that Act. There have been substantial changes in procedure, principally the abolition of the bankruptcy notice and 'acts of bankruptcy' and the replacement of the receiving and adjudication orders by a single bankruptcy order. A creditor may bring bankruptcy proceedings if the debtor owes him £750 or more (ss.264, 267). Unless his petition is based on an unsatisfied execution of a judgment or order of a court, he must have served a 'statutory demand' in prescribed form at least 3 weeks before filing his petition, unless there is a serious risk of diminution of the debtor's property during that period (ss.268, 270). The matter then proceeds to a hearing, when a bankruptcy order may be made by the court, having broadly the same effect as an adjudication order under the previous law. A bankrupt will normally obtain his discharge automatically three years after the making of the bankruptcy order (s.279).

6.187 Section 1(1)(g) of the Bankruptcy Act 1914 was repealed by the Insolvency Act 1985 and was not re-enacted. Section 383(1) of the Insolvency Act 1986 defines a 'creditor' (who, subject to the Act's provisions, may present a bankruptcy petition under section 264, *ibid.*) as a person to whom a bankruptcy debt is owed. However, the last sentence of this paragraph in the main text may also apply to enforcement by bankruptcy.

Rectification of accounts

6.194 Both in *Stockdale* v. *Haringey L.B.C.* (6.32A, above) and *Hazell* v. *Hammersmith and Fulham L.B.C.* (6.22C, above) the court ordered rectification of accounts with liberty to the parties to apply to the court if appropriate rectification could not be agreed.

CHAPTER 7

MISCONDUCT AND FAILURE TO BRING INTO ACCOUNT

I CERTIFICATION OF SUMS DUE

7.1   Section 20 of the Local Government Finance Act 1982, as amended, does not apply to the audit of health service bodies (National Health Service and Community Care Act 1990, Sch.4, para.10). But see 5.6B-C, above, as to responsibility of the health service auditor in respect of unlawful decisions involving the possibility of unlawful expenditure or of loss or deficiency.

7.2   The opinion expressed in the penultimate sentence of this paragraph was confirmed by the Divisional Court in *Fleming* v. *Lees*, [1991] C.O.D. 50. The auditor found that an objector had made a *prima facie* case that he should certify a sum due from councillors for loss due to wilful misconduct in respect of the costs incurred in resisting an earlier application for judicial review by the objector. The auditor accordingly gave the councillors concerned an opportunity to answer the case. The sum was then paid in on behalf of the councillors. The objector argued that the auditor should nevertheless certify the sum due from the councillors because it was due at the date to which the accounts were made up. The auditor refused to do so and the objector appealed. The court held that since the auditor is required by section 20(1) of the Local Government Finance Act 1982 to certify that a sum *is* due he must focus on whether there is a loss at the date of certification or refusal to certify; to deny the force of the present tense would produce the absurdities: (a) of a distinction between recoupment in the financial year and one after the end of the year; and (b) of the possibility of double recoupment. For other aspects of this case see 7.61D, 9.17, below.

III LOSS DUE TO WILFUL MISCONDUCT

Wilful misconduct

7.42   In *Lloyd* v. *McMahon*, [1987] A.C. 625 (7.61A-C, below) the House of Lords made it clear that in case of wilful failure to carry out statutory duty, or to carry it out without unreasonable delay, sincerity of motive would not excuse such failure or prevent it being held to be wilful misconduct (pp.696H, 713C-714A).

Loss through waste

7.50A   As to the conditions to be satisfied before an auditor could allege loss due to wilful misconduct in failing to take action to avoid waste which he may have identified in a previous report, see 4.77A, above.

Causation - intervening causes

7.55,n.24 Reference to McGregor, *Damages*, is applicable also to 15th edn.

Failure to raise income as required by law

7.58   Section 111, Housing Act 1957, has been replaced on consolidation by section 24, Housing Act 1985.

7.58-61 The substance of these paragraphs applies to the setting of community charges under section 32 of the Local Government Finance Act 1988 as it applied to the levy of rates under the General Rate Act 1967. So do the decisions referred to at paragraphs 7.61A to 7.61D, below, subject to the distinction that there is an express requirement that community charges must be set on or before 1 April (s.32(2)). (There was no such express requirement for rates in the year to which the cases following relate).

7.61A In *Smith* v. *Skinner, Gladden* v. *McMahon* (1986), 26 R.V.R. 45, the Divisional Court upheld decisions of district auditors to certify sums due from members of Lambeth L.B.C. and Liverpool City Council in respect of losses due to their wilful misconduct in delaying the making of rates for the year ended 31 March 1986 until 24 July 1985 and 14 June 1985 respectively. The amounts certified due, over £100,000 in each case, were made up of interest on delayed rate rebate subsidy and delayed payment of rates on Crown property; delayed rate income was unquantifiable at the date of the auditors' calculation of the sums to be certified due.

7.61B The court dismissed appeals by members of both councils against the auditors' decisions, holding in each case:

(1)   that the councils' decisions to defer making a rate were made with the improper object of putting pressure on the Secretary of State to provide increased funds from central government, and were therefore unlawful;

(2)   that in wilfully disregarding advice to that effect from their officers and the district auditors, the councillors showed that they knew, or at least were recklessly indifferent to, the fact that they were acting wrongly, and were therefore guilty of wilful misconduct;

(3)   that the misconduct caused the losses as calculated by the auditors.

The court rejected submissions by the appellants that the auditors had acted unfairly in inviting representations from the councillors in writing rather than orally and in allegedly introducing into their statements of reasons matters on which the appellants had not been given an opportunity to comment.

7.61C On appeal by the Liverpool councillors to the Court of Appeal and the House of Lords, *sub nom. Lloyd* v. *McMahon*, [1987] A.C. 625, the reasoning of the Divisional Court as indicated under heads (1) to (3) of the foregoing paragraph was upheld. On the questions whether the auditor had acted unfairly the Court of Appeal had reservations as to whether an oral hearing should have been offered, but it was held that any unfairness there may have been was cured by the appeal to the Divisional Court. The House of Lords unanimously rejected the allegations of unfairness, holding that in the circumstances of the case fairness did not require the offer of an oral hearing and that the matters relied on by the auditor in his statement of reasons were broadly covered in an earlier notice by the auditor to the councillors on which they had commented in writing. For further details of the decisions on the question of oral hearings see 10.36A-C, below.

7.61D Delay in rate-making was also the subject of *Fleming* v. *Lees*, [1991] C.O.D. 50, in which an objector unsuccessfully appealed against the auditor's refusal to certify a sum due in respect of loss caused to Hackney L.B.C. by alleged wilful misconduct in not levying a rate until 22 May 1985. The objector had previously instituted judicial review proceedings against the council which had resulted in the issue of an order of mandamus dated 16 April 1985 commanding the council to make a rate by 31 May 1985 (*R.* v. *Hackney L.B.C., ex parte Fleming* (1985), 85 L.G.R. 626). In his appeal against the auditor's decision, the objector argued that the order of mandamus established that the council were in breach of duty at least from the date of that order, and that the breach of duty was occasioned by wilful misconduct of councillors. In preliminary proceedings it was ordered that the hearing of the appeal should be divided into stages and that stage one should deal with the question whether there had been a breach of duty as alleged. At the hearing of stage one the Divisional Court held that the council were not in breach of duty in not making a rate until 22 May 1985; the issue of the order of mandamus did not imply an extant breach of duty and there was nothing in the judgment in the judicial review proceedings to suggest that there was or would be a breach of duty (at least before 31 May 1985). For other aspects of this case see 7.2, above, 9.17, below.

Disqualification

7.62   After the decision of the Divisional Court in *Smith* v. *Skinner, Gladden* v. *McMahon* (7.61A, above), counsel for the auditor asked the court if they agreed that the auditor's certificate and the consequent disqualification of councillors would not take effect, under section 20(4), until either the end of the 28 days after judgment allowed for appeal, if no appeal notice had then been entered, or otherwise at such time as an appeal to the Court of Appeal was finally disposed of. It was accepted, said counsel, that it was not a matter for the court to determine that day, but the parties would be grateful for any advice that could be given. Glidewell L.J. said that the court's tentative view was that the granting of leave to appeal would operate as a stay pending the entry of a notice of appeal, but if leave to appeal were not to be given then other results might follow (Transcript, Marten Walsh Cherer Ltd., CO/1474-1553/85, p.189). The latter question did not arise in this case because leave to appeal was given by the Divisional Court. But it would seem logical that if that were not so, it would follow that the appeal could not be regarded as 'finally disposed of', and that the certificate and disqualification would not therefore be operative, until time had expired for application to the Court of Appeal for leave to appeal.

Auditors' duties as to fraud, etc.

7.63   For changes in the section on fraud etc. in the 1990 Code of Audit Practice see 4.24, above.

7.64   Paragraph 39 of the 1983 Code is repeated without change of substance in paragraph 33 of the 1990 Code.

IV   ASSESSMENT OF SUMS CERTIFIED DUE

Use of broad estimates

7.66,n.29   Reference to McGregor, *Damages,* is applicable also to 15th edn.

Adjustment for incidental matters

Interest

7.67   In last line, add to passage in brackets 'inserting new s.35A, Supreme Court Act 1981; County Courts Act 1984, s.69'.

7.69-72 In *Smith* v. *Skinner, Gladden* v. *McMahon*, 7.61A, above, the sums certified due were based entirely on loss of interest due to wilful misconduct in delaying the making of rates. It was not argued by the appellants at any stage that 'loss or deficiency' in section 20 of the 1982 did not include a loss of interest.

V RECOVERY OF SUMS CERTIFIED DUE

Action for recovery

7.78   Action for recovery of sums certified due, being for money recoverable by statute, is now within the jurisdiction of the county court whatever the amount involved (County Courts Act 1984, s.16; High Court and County Courts Jurisdiction Order 1991, S.I. 724, art.2(1)(1)). Actions in which the plaintiff reasonably expects to recover either less than £25,000 or more than £50,000 are to be tried in the county court or High Court respectively unless either court considers otherwise, having regard to specified criteria (*ibid.*, arts.7, 9). Enforcement of county court judgments by execution against goods must be effected in the High Court if for £5,000 or more and may be so effected if for £2,000 or more (*ibid.*, art.8).

Procedure

7.80   The County Court (Amendment No.4) Rules 1989 (S.I. 1989/2426) substitute Order 17, rule 11, of the County Court Rules so that pre-trial reviews will no longer be held in ordinary default actions and automatic directions apply to such matters as the periods of time allowed for discovery of documents and requests for a hearing.

7.81   Interest is also payable on costs awarded by the High Court from the date of pronouncement of judgment: *Hunt* v. *R.M. Douglas (Roofing) Ltd.*, [1990] 1 A.C.398.

In note 37, for 'r.8(6)' read 'r.8(4)'.

Time

7.82   Further as to the meaning of 'finally disposed of' in section 20(5) of the 1982 Act, see 7.62, above.

Compensation orders by criminal courts

7.84   The sentences from lines 9 to 12 should be amended to read:

'In civil proceedings for the same loss the damages must be assessed without regard to the order, but the plaintiff may only recover the aggregate of: (a) any amount by which the damages exceed the compensation; and (b) any compensation which he fails to recover, and may not enforce the latter without the leave of the court (s.38(2)), as substituted by s.105, Criminal Justice Act 1988).'

Recovery from superannuation fund

7.85-6 References to regulations L13, L16 and 17 of the Local Government Superannuation Regulations 1974 should now be replaced by references to regulations M1, M2 and M3 respectively of the Local Government Superannuation Regulations 1986 (S.I. 1986/24). In line 10 of 7.86 for 'S.I 1978/266, reg.12(3)(b)' read 'S.I. 1986/24, reg.E29(1)(b)'.

Replace n.39 by 'Regs.M2(4), C12(9)-(11)'. In n.40, replace 'S.I. 1977/1845, reg.4' by 'Reg.M1(1)(c)'. In n.41, replace reference to regulations by 'Regs.M2(4)(b), C12(9)-(11)'. The reference to S.I. 1978/266 in n.42 is no longer required. In n.44, for references to reg.C8 and its amendments read 'reg.C12'.

CHAPTER 8

PUBLIC RIGHTS

I INTRODUCTION – PRELIMINARIES

8.1   Sections 17 and 23 of the Local Government Finance Act 1982, as amended, do not apply to the audit of health service bodies (National Health Service and Community Care Act 1990, Sch.4, paras.7, 13).

8.3   In last two lines, for 'paras.11, 12' of Code of Audit Practice, read 'paras.68, 69/1990'.

Public notice of rights

8.6   The error in the regulations referred to in lines 4 to 11 was corrected by the Accounts and Audit (Amendment) Regulations 1986, S.I. 1986/1271. Regulation 11(3) as amended provides for notice to be displayed 'for a period of at least 14 days immediately prior to the period during which the accounts and other documents are made available under regulation 9'.

II INSPECTION OF ACCOUNTS AND DOCUMENTS

Documents available for inspection

8.18   The Local Government (Access to Information) Act 1985 inserted a new part VA (ss.100A-100K) in the Local Government Act 1972, widening public access to minutes and other papers relating to meetings of local authorities. Except for minutes of periods when the public were excluded which disclose exempt information (as defined in s.100I and Sch.12A), minutes of principal councils (including joint authorities, etc., - s.100J) and committees and sub-committees thereof, and agendas, reports and background papers relating thereto, are open to inspection by members of the public for four years in the case of background papers and six years for the remainder (ss.100C-100E). Section 228(1) of the 1972 Act still applies to parish and community councils.

8.20A   In *Oliver* v. *Northampton B.C.* (1986), 151 J.P. 44, it was held that a wages book or its computerised equivalent was open to inspection under section 17 of the 1982 Act, its confidentiality being irrelevant. The effect was that details of employees' tax and national insurance payments, and where applicable attachment of earnings orders, could be disclosed. The court criticised the section as too sweeping in this respect, and section 11 of the Local Government and Housing Act 1989 (App.A.3, below) subsequently restricted it so as not to allow inspection of personal information about a member of staff which is available to the body in connection with his employment, or to require such information to be disclosed in answer to any question (see also 8.27-8, below). The restriction extends to information available to the body in respect of payments or benefits provided by the body in connection with any office or employment under any other person (subs.(2)(b)) or in connection with the cessation of any office or employment (subs.(3)).

8.20B It appears that computer-produced reports which would fall within section 17(1) if produced manually are not restricted from inspection by the Data Protection Act 1984, since section 34(1) thereof provides exemption from the Act as a whole when the user is required by enactment to make personal data available to the public by making it available for inspection.

III   QUESTIONING THE AUDITOR

Local government electors - representatives

8.25A The question has been raised whether section 17 could be interpreted as meaning that anyone - not necessarily a local government elector - could himself ask questions or make objections, provided he has a piece of paper signed by a local government elector appointing him to do so. Jowitt's Dictionary of English Law defines 'representative' as 'a person who represents or takes the place of another', and in *R. v. Greenwich County Court Registrar* (1885), 15 Q.B.D. 54, 58, Brett M.R. drew a distinction between counsel acting in court, who 'has the whole conduct of the cause and... the power to act without asking his client what he shall do' and a solicitor, who 'represents his client in court and... represents him out of court. He acts for him, and in his own name, and therefore in ordinary legal language he is the representative of his client'. (Thus for the purpose of the Bankruptcy Act 1883, which required a creditor's representative to be authorised in writing, counsel was not the 'representative' of the creditor, but a solicitor was.)

8.25B Following this guidance, it appears that the function of a representative is that he represents, or acts for, his principal and that he has no rights other than those deputed to him by his principal; under section 17 of the 1982 Act he can therefore ask questions only to elicit information which his principal has authorised him to seek and can only make objections which his principal has authorised him to make. (This would appear to apply also to a barrister, who would in this case be appearing as a representative under the statute rather than under his inherent rights in court as in the *Greenwich* case.) This conclusion accords with that in 8.25, main text, that the evident intention of section 17 is to equate the right to question and object with the right to vote.

Limitations on the right to question

8.27-8 In line 5 of 8.27 and lines 1 and 10 of 8.28, for 'paragraph 15' of the Code of Audit Practice read 'paragraph 71/1990'. The 1990 paragraph adds that the auditor should not disclose personal information about the remuneration or other benefits paid to a member of the authority's staff (see 8.20A, above).

IV   OBJECTIONS AT AUDIT

8.36-7 For references to 'paragraph 16' of the Code of Audit Practice read 'paragraph 72/1990'.

8.40,41,n.10 For references to Supreme Court Practice, read '1991, 18/19/17'.

8.41,42,n.11 For '1985' edition of Supreme Court Practice, read '1991'.

Attendance at the audit

8.43   As to the position of a representative of a local government elector making objections to the accounts, see 8.25A-B, above.

On the question whether the provision for attendance before the auditor confers a right to an oral hearing, see main text 10.37 and 10.37A-B, below.

As to the delegation by the auditor of the hearing of objections, see 2.71, above.

V   OTHER REMEDIES

The relator action

8.46,n.13 For 'p.532' of *Wade,* read '(6th edn.), p.605'.

Judicial review

8.49-52 As to application by auditors for judicial review, see 5.41Q-W, above. For judicial review of auditors' decisions, see main text 9.35-6 and 9.36A-D, below.

8.50,n.17 For 'pp.551-563' of *Wade,* read '(6th edn.), pp.630- 643'.

8.51   In line 10, for 'pp.582-5' of *Wade,* read '(6th edn.), pp.694-7'.

As to the grant of interim relief by the court, see 5.41R, above, which applies generally to applications for judicial review.

8.51, n.18 For 'p.588, pp.551-563' of *Wade,* read '(6th edn.) p.702, pp.688-709'.

8.52,n.19 For 'p.590' of *Wade,* read '(6th edn.), p.705'.

8.52,n.20 Section 4 of the Local Government Finance Act 1982 has no operation in respect of financial years from 1990/1 onwards (Local Government Finance Act 1988, s.117). Grounds of appeal against community charges are set out in section 23(2) of the 1988 Act. Community Charge Practice Note No.7 dated 3 October 1988 (prepared jointly by D.O.E./W.O. and the local authority associations) points out that the setting of charges and precepts is not subject to appeal under that section and may only be questioned by judicial review (para.2.4).

8.52A In *R. v. Westminster City Council, ex parte Hilditch, The Independent,* 26 June 1990, the Court of Appeal refused leave to apply for judicial review of the council's decisions on the ground that the applicant had already objected at audit on the same subject-matter, the objection being still under investigation by the auditor. In the circumstances of the case, the court held that there were no grounds of urgency to justify judicial review and that the audit remedy was more apt to decide disputed issues of fact. The normal rule thus applied, that an applicant who had invoked a statutory remedy should first exhaust his rights under that remedy.

CHAPTER 9

APPLICATIONS AND APPEALS

I COURTS HAVING JURISDICTION

Limits of county court jurisdiction

9.2-4   These paragraphs of the main text (except for the last three sentences of para.9.4) are superseded as a result of the High Court and County Courts Jurisdiction Order 1991, S.I. 724, which provides that county courts shall have jurisdiction under sections 19 and 20 of the Local Government Finance Act 1982, whatever the amount involved in the proceedings (art.2(1)(k)). Applications under section 19 and appeals under section 20 must be commenced in the High Court (art.6), but the High Court may transfer them to a county court for trial, having regard to criteria of financial substance, importance (including importance to non-parties and in the public interest), complexity and speed of trial (art.7(5)). It appears that article 6 does not cover appeals by objectors under section 19(4) and that these may therefore be commenced in a county court, but may be transferred to the High Court at the discretion of either the county court or the High Court, having regard to the above criteria of article 7(5).

Paragraph (3) of article 7 provides that actions of which the value is less than £25,000 shall be tried in a county court unless the High Court considers, having regard to the said criteria, that it ought to try the action. Paragraph (4) provides, subject to a corresponding condition, that actions of value more than £50,000 shall be tried in the High Court. The value of an action is defined by article 9 to be its financial worth to the plaintiff or applicant (no mention of appellants, but they may perhaps be included in applicants). Paragraphs (3) and (4) do not apply to actions of no such quantifiable value (art.7(2)). The application of paragraphs (3) and (4) to proceedings under section 19 is therefore questionable since neither an applicant auditor nor an appellant objector would have any, or any quantifiable, personal financial interest in the result. However the court has in any case a discretion, subject to regard to the specified criteria (including financial substance) and the matter will no doubt be so determined, whether or not paragraphs (3) and (4) apply.

9.6   Since applications under sections 19 and appeals under section 20 of the 1982 Act must all now be made to the High Court (9.2-4, above), it appears that paragraphs (1) to (6) of C.C.R., O.49, r.10 are now applicable only to appeal by objectors under section 19(4).

II APPLICATIONS TO THE COURT

High Court

Parties

9.11   In *Hazell* v. *Hammersmith and Fulham L.B.C.* (6.22C, above), banks involved in the transactions in question were allowed to be joined as parties to the proceedings. The questions arising on this issue were the subject of comment in the Divisional Court judgment, at [1990] 2 Q.B. 697, 733. Woolf L.J. said that any declaration which the court made would not affect third parties and referred to the refusal to allow the contractor to be joined in *Re Hurle-Hobbs*. But this did not mean, he said, that it was not right for the banks to be represented in the present case; these proceedings were unusual in that the council conceded that they were acting *ultra vires* and it was important that the banks should be able to put forward arguments for taking a different view from the auditor and the council in order to minimise the possibility of conflict between decisions of this court and decisions in possible future proceedings between the council and the banks. In the House of Lords Lord Templeman said merely 'A decision that all the transactions were unlawful could have serious financial repercussions on the banks... The banks have therefore joined in these proceedings' ([1991] 2 W.L.R. 373, 377).

County Court

9.12   See 9.2-4, 9.6, above.

III   APPEALS FROM AUDITORS

Rights of appeal

9.16   In the penultimate sentence, for 'para.20' read 'para.77/1990'.

9.17   In *Fleming* v. *Lees,* [1991] C.O.D. 50, an appeal by an objector against an auditor's refusal to certify sums due, the auditor submitted, *inter alia,* that the court, even if it found against him on the merits, could not in the circumstances of the case give a certificate under section 20(3) of the 1982 Act, because the auditor himself could not have given a certificate on the date of his decision not to certify. The auditor's inability to certify was put on the basis that in the circumstances described at 7.61D, above, he had not heard any representations by or on behalf of the councillors, though he had told them that he would give them an opportunity to be heard before coming to a decision against them. The court, while dismissing the objector's appeal, rejected the auditor's submission on this point. It was held that the court, in the exercise of its wide powers under section 20(3), could in these circumstances rehear the matter (or perhaps remit it) and then (if appropriate) issue the certificate which the auditor could have issued after hearing the councillors (Transcript, pp.18-20; this point is not covered in the C.O.D. report).

Statements of reasons

9.18   In *William Hill Organisation Ltd.* v. *Gavas,* [1990] 2 Admin. L.R. 701, an employer who wished to appeal against an industrial tribunal decision of unfair dismissal did not ask for a full statement of reasons until a month after expiry of the 21 days after the decision allowed for such a request. The request was refused and the Employment Appeal Tribunal subsequently held that it was impossible to adjudicate on the appeal in the absence of full reasons. The Court of Appeal dismissed an appeal against this decision, holding that the refusal to provide full reasons was within the discretion of the industrial tribunal and that it was impossible to overrule the conclusion of the E.A.T. that the appeal was not justiciable in the absence of full reasons.

9.18,n.9   Paragraph 77, 1990 Code of Audit Practice, provides that a statement of reasons is normally to be sent to the objector by recorded delivery.

9.19-20   For 'para.20' of the Code of Audit Practice in the last line of each paragraph, read 'para.77/1990'.

9.21　For 'para.24(f)' of the Code of Audit Practice towards the end of the paragraph, read 'para.58(k)/1990'.

Procedure on appeal

9.22　R.S.C. Order 98 has no application to appeals against prohibition orders under section 25B of the Local Government Finance Act 1982, which are therefore governed by Orders 55 and 57.

9.24　In line 6, after 'disqualification', add 'or rectification of accounts'.

9.26　See 9.6, above.

9.28,n.13　For '1985' edition of *Supreme Court Practice*, read '1991'.

Judicial review

9.36,nn.18-21　For references to *Wade* read: n.18, 'pp.945-7'; n.19, 'pp.712-3, 945-7'; n.20, 'pp.628-9'; n.21, 'pp.311 ff.' (all 6th edn.).

9.36A　In *Smith* v. *Skinner, Gladden* v. *McMahon* (1986), 26 R.V.R. 45 (7.61A, above), counsel for the auditor submitted that it was not open to the councillors, in an appeal under section 20(3) of the Local Government Finance Act 1982, to challenge the validity of an auditor's decision on grounds of unfair procedure, the correct procedure for such a challenge being by way of judicial review. Glidewell L.J., at p.55, considered that in principle this was so, but that he was bound by the Court of Appeal decision in *Asher* v. *Secretary of State for the Environment*, [1974] Ch. 208 (main text, 9.36,n.18). But the Court of Appeal, in *Lloyd* v. *McMahon*, [1987] A.C. 625, held that it was correctly decided in *Asher* that a challenge to the fairness of an auditor's procedure was within the scope of an appeal under the 1982 Act; they further considered that such challenges ought to be made by way of appeal and not by judicial review (pp.653F, 676C). In the House of Lords, Lord Bridge said that an auditor's certificate could no doubt be the subject of application for judicial review, but could see no reason for that when an aggrieved party was entitled to the ampler rights of statutory appeal (p.709A). Lord Keith agreed (p.697G).

9.36B　In *R.* v. *District Auditor, No.10 Audit District, ex parte Judge, The Times*, 26 December 1988, an objection had been dismissed by the auditor without an oral hearing. The objector did not appeal under section 19(4) of the 1982 Act but applied for leave to seek judicial review on the ground of failure to allow him to attend the audit to make oral representations under section 17(3) of that Act. Leave was granted, *ex parte*, on the basis of written evidence; the auditor applied to set aside the grant of leave on the ground, *inter alia*, that on the authority of *Lloyd* v. *McMahon* the objector should have raised it by appeal under section 19(4) and not by judicial review. Rose J. held that *Lloyd* v. *McMahon* applied to section 19 no less than to section 20, and for this reason, among others, set aside the grant of leave (Transcript, Marten Walsh Cherer Ltd., pp.12C, 13F). On dismissing an appeal, the Court of Appeal approved this reason as the principal reason for the decision (Transcript, Association of Official Shorthandwriters Ltd., p.4E).

Judicial review of auditor's report

9.36C　Three cases have been before the courts in which local authorities have sought judicial review of statements in audit reports under section 15 of the Local Government Finance Act 1982 questioning the legality of action proposed by the authorities. In *R.* v. *District Auditor No.3 Audit District, ex parte West Yorkshire Metropolitan C.C.* (1985), 26 R.V.R.

24 (6.146A, above), the Divisional Court expressed doubts whether judicial review was an appropriate remedy, since the auditor had made no determination, the views expressed in his report being no more than provisional. But as both parties agreed that there was a point of substance which needed to be determined quickly the court agreed to hear the case without creating a precedent as to correct procedure for the future, and issued a declaration that the action proposed by the authority was invalid. In *R.* v. *District Auditor for Leicester, ex parte Leicester City Council* (1985), 25 R.V.R. 191 (6.145-6, above), both parties accepted that the court had jurisdiction, and Woolf J., after considering the judgment in the *West Yorkshire* case, agreed to deal with the application because of the considerable inconvenience which would otherwise be caused, but expressed the view that if the court had a jurisdiction it was one that should be sparingly exercised and only when there was a real dispute between the parties as to a limited issue (p.193). The Court of Appeal also agreed that the matter should be dealt with (29 R.V.R., p.163).

9.36D Each of the above cases arose before auditors themselves had the power to apply for judicial review conferred by the Local Government Act 1988 (5.41Q, above), and the auditor had in each case accepted that the court should hear the application for judicial review in order that the matter should be dealt with expeditiously. In *R.* v. *Arthur Young (a firm), ex parte Thamesdown B. C., The Independent*, 16 February 1989, the auditor opposed the principle of his report being attacked by judicial review. In the report he had urged the council to refrain from proceeding with a factoring agreement for the sale of the rights to receipts from future sales of land, pending a decision of the courts, on an application for judicial review by another auditor, on the legality of such agreements (*R.* v. *Wirral M.B.C., ex parte Milstead*, 6.22A above). The Thamesdown council applied for judicial review, asking for an order of certiorari to quash what was alleged to be a decision of the auditor and for a declaration that their proposed factoring agreement was lawful. Leave to apply was granted *ex parte* but the auditor applied for the leave granted to be set aside, arguing that he had made no decision capable of being subject to certiorari and that section 31(2), Supreme Court Act 1981, did not permit a declaration being made on judicial review where no prerogative order was available. Pill J. held that the claim for certiorari was, on the available material, hopeless, and that there was considerable force in the auditor's submissions questioning entitlement to a declaration, but that the court should not defeat the purpose of the leave procedure by going into the matter in any great depth. So leave would not be set aside, the matter being left to be determined at the substantive hearing. By the time that the substantive hearing came on, however, judgment had been given in the *Wirral* case and it was conceded by the Thamesdown council that that judgment defeated their substantive case on the factoring agreement. The procedural question whether they were entitled to seek judicial review of the auditor's report was not therefore considered by the court.

IV   APPEAL TO HIGHER COURTS

Court of Appeal

9.38,n.22 For reference to *Supreme Court Practice*, read '1991, 59/3/4'.

9.40, 41   For '1985' edition of *Supreme Court Practice*, read '1991'.

V̇ COSTS AND EXPENSES

Appeals and applications

9.45,n.24 The 'common fund' and 'party-party' bases for taxation of costs were super-seded in 1986. The current bases are the 'standard' basis, on which a reasonable amount is to be allowed in respect of costs reasonably incurred, any doubts as to reasonableness being resolved in favour of the paying party; and the 'indemnity' basis, on which all costs are allowed except insofar as they are of unreasonable amount or have been unreasonably incurred, any doubts as to reasonableness being resolved in favour of the receiving party. Costs are taxed on the standard basis unless the court specifies the indemnity basis (R.S.C., O.62., r.12).

9.47A Orders were made by the court for payment by the authority of the auditor's net expenses under section 19(5) or 20(7) of the 1982 Act in *Wilkinson* v. *Doncaster M.B.C.* (C.A. - 6.2, above), *Lloyd* v. *McMahon* (C.A. - 7.61C), *Hemsted* v. *Lees* (Q.B. - 6.44), *Stockdale* v. *Haringey L.B.C.* (D.C. and C.A. - 6.32A), *R.* v. *Wirral M.B.C, ex parte Milstead* (D.C. - 6.22A), *Fleming* v. Lees (D.C. - 7.2, 7.61D), and *Hazell* v. *Hammersmith and Fulham L.B.C.* (D.C. - 6.22E). No such orders were made in *Lloyd* (D.C. and H.L.), in *Hazell* (C.A. and H.L.), or in *R.* v. *District Auditor and Northants C.C., ex parte Gray* (Q.B. - 9.47C).

9.47B In most of the above cases the orders were made or refused with little or no comment. In *Lloyd* v. *McMahon*, in the Court of Appeal, Lawton L.J. said:

> 'It seems to me, Mr Cross, that when we come to exercise such discretion as we have under subsection 7 we must not deal with it arbitrarily, we must deal with it on principle; and on the face of it Parliament intended that the expenses incurred in connection with an appeal should be paid by the local authority to which the appeal relates. That was clearly, I would have thought, the intention of Parliament. What you are really saying is that Liverpool is in such a bad state at the present time that it is just bad luck on them that they should incur these extra expenses. But is that, as a matter of law, a good ground for exercising our discretion?
>
> ...
>
> Discretion must be used on right principles, you know. We are not supposed to exercise our discretion taking into account matters we ought not to take into account; and is it a right exercise of discretion to say that the cost of all this should fall upon other ratepayers all over the country and not on Liverpool, because Liverpool is in a parlous condition?' (Transcript, Association of Official Shorthandwriters Ltd., p.87).

The House of Lords did not overrule the Court of Appeal's order as to the expenses in that court, but made no order as to the expenses of the House of Lords case. Lord Keith of Kinkel said only 'This is a suitable case for directing, under section 20(7) of the Act of 1982, that any unrecovered costs shall not be paid by the city of Liverpool' ([1987] A.C. 625, 698).

9.47C In *Hemsted* v. *Lees*, McCowan J. said:

> 'As Mr Elvin points out, there is the provision which gives a court the power to make the order which he seeks and in this case the District Auditor has sought to protect the ratepayers of Norwich by resisting the appeal. He has done so successfully. I can see no good reason why he should not get such expenses as he has, over and above the costs which he recovers from the unsuccessful appellant, from the Local Authority in question. In consequence, I grant the application' (Transcript, Marten Walsh Cherer Ltd., CO/406/85, p.25).

This decision was cited and followed in *Fleming* v. *Lees*. It was not cited in *R.* v. *District Auditor and Northants C.C., ex parte Gray*, 20 July 1988, unreported. In that case the objector had also challenged the council's action directly in the courts, and when that challenge was dismissed had abandoned his appeal against the auditor's decision on the same subject-matter. Henry J. said that the objector's challenge was misconceived and hopeless and he declined to make an order for expenses against the council because he considered it more just that the burden of such a misconceived appeal should be spread nationwide rather than on an individual county (Transcript, Marten Walsh Cherer Ltd., CO/1430/87, p.8).

9.47D In *Hazell* v. *Hammersmith and Fulham L.B.C.* the House of Lords decided that the order of the Divisional Court for payment by the council of the auditor's net expenses in that court should stand, but that no such order should be made in respect of the further appeals, 'since the council was not responsible for the appeal to the Court of Appeal or the appeal to this House and since the appeal dealt with questions of general importance' ([1991] 2 W.L.R. 372, 397E).

9.47E Some variation appeared in reaction of the courts to the question, in cases where it was raised, of how to deal with any disagreement on the amount of the auditor's expenses. In *Hemsted* v. *Lees*, the court followed Nolan J. in *Wilkinson* v. *Doncaster M.B.C.* (main text, 9.46) in giving liberty to apply to the court. But the Court of Appeal in the *Doncaster* case ordered that the amount of expenses, in default of agreement, should be determined by the taxing master, and this was followed in *Fleming* v. *Lees*.

Costs payable by party and by authority

9.49 In *Lloyd* v. *McMahon*, where there were 47 appellants, some legally aided and some not, the House of Lords ordered each appellant to pay one forty-seventh of the auditor's costs, subject to the usual protection afforded by the legal aid certificates, and added that if and so far as the auditor did not recover a due proportion from a legally aided appellant and subject to any application by the Law Society, the auditor should be entitled to recover from the legal aid fund pursuant to section 13 of the Legal Aid Act 1974.

Security for costs

9.50,n.26 For reference to Supreme Court Practice, read '1991, 59/10/19,20'.

Costs of the authority

9.51 In *Hemsted* v. *Lees*, the appellant was ordered to pay the auditor's costs but not those of the council. McCowan J. said:

> 'It is common ground that the local authority has the right to appear. It has chosen to do so, but it is also common ground that it is usually necessary to show special reasons for appearance by the authority if they are to have their costs... I quite accept that the authority for whom he appeared might want to be represented, but that does not appear to me to be the test... In this case the authority accepted and supported all of the auditor's reasons. I therefore find it impossible to say that it is a case where there are special reasons for the authority's appearance' (Transcript, Marten Walsh Cherer Ltd., CO/406/85, p.22).

Costs were awarded both to the auditor and the council against the appellant in *Fleming* v. *Lees*. Reasons stated by the court were only that it was entirely proper for the council to be represented and that no reason could be seen why the unsuccessful appellant should not pay the costs of the auditor and the council. In submission on behalf of the council it had been accepted that two sets of costs were not generally awarded without special reasons, but submitted that in this case the council had felt it necessary to be represented because: (i) the conduct of the council had been in issue; (ii) orders for discovery had been made against it; (iii) new evidence had been submitted by the appellant (Transcript, CO/780/ 88, pp.25-6).

In *R.* v. *District Auditor and Northants C.C., ex parte Gray,* costs were not awarded to the council on the ground that the objector's belated realism in abandoning the appeal should be reflected in tempering the order for costs against him.

CHAPTER 10

PROCEDURAL AND GENERAL MATTERS

This chapter relates almost entirely to the special powers of the local government auditor under sections 19 and 20 of the Local Government Finance Act 1982 and therefore has little application to health service audits, which are, however, mentioned in paragraphs 10.17 and 10.57.

I NATURE OF AUDITOR'S DUTIES - JUDICIAL OR OTHERWISE

10.2   For references to *Wade*, 'pp.438, 450, 465',read '(6th edn.), pp.492, 505-6, 522-3'.

10.4-6,nn.1,3 For references to *Wade*, 'pp.781, 787, 824, 822', read '(6th edn.), pp.899, 906, 948, 945'.

10.12-16   In *Lloyd* v. *McMahon*, [1987] A.C. 625, 664D-F, Woolf L.J. said:

'Both under section 19 and under section 20... the same initial requirement is laid down by the statute, namely that 'it appears to the auditor'.... Whether the auditor is acting under section 19 or section 20, his role is at least in part inquisitorial. While he would always be under an obligation to look fairly into the objection and deal fairly with any person who can be affected by his decision, both under section 19 and under section 20 his role is not identical to that of a judge in court'.

This *dictum* was issued in the context of the question whether there should be a requirement for an oral hearing having regard to the auditor's function under section 20. Woolf L.J. had earlier referred to the auditor's function under the category of 'a quasi-judicial function of this sort' and expressed the view that such a case warranted the application of a 'general requirement of fairness' rather than a 'rigid requirement for an oral hearing' (p.663E-G).

10.17 The local government auditor's new function of issuing prohibition orders (5.41A-P, above) is evidently of a similar nature, under this heading, to his function under section 20 (main text, 10.12). In issuing a prohibition order the auditor bears some similarity to a court in that he makes an initial decision with legal effect, subject to appeal. In applying for judicial review, however (5.41Q-S), he merely brings a question before the court for decision, and since objectors play no part in this process, the arguments in favour of section 19 action by the auditor being possibly regarded as quasi-judicial (main text, 10.14-16) have no application to the question of judicial review.

The health service auditor's duty, in cases which he has reason to believe involve illegal expenditure or loss or deficiency (5.6B, above) is only to act as an intermediary in referring the matter to the Secretary of State and can hardly be regarded as quasi-judicial in character.

II NATURAL JUSTICE

10.18,n.4 For 'pp.423-6, 447-68', of *Wade*, read '(6th edn.),pp.475-8, 502-26'.

The rule against bias

10.19 In fourth last line, for 'para.14' of the Code of Audit Practice', read 'para.70/1990'.

10.19,nn.6,8,9 For references to *Wade*, 'pp.421-6, 430, 434-5', read '(6th edn.), pp.473-8, 482, 488-9'.

10.21A In *British Muslims Association* v. *Secretary of State for the Environment* (1988), 55 P. & C.R. 205, a compulsory purchase order was quashed because the inspector at the inquiry into the order held a conversation for an appreciable time with officers of the council in the absence of the owners and tenants of the property. It was held that the proper test for bias was whether a reasonable observer might conclude that a procedural unfairness indicative of bias had occurred so as to vitiate the fairness necessary in the conduct of quasi-judicial functions; and that while there was on the facts no actual impropriety, an inference of impropriety might be drawn. A similar decision was made in *Simmons* v. *Secretary of State for the Environment,* [1985] J.P.L. 253. In considering the significance of such cases for the auditor due weight must be given, as indicated in main text, paragraphs 10.21 and 10.33, to the investigatory role of the auditor, but the cases may be considered to emphasise the need for caution as to the auditor's personal contacts with the parties where his quasi-judicial role is concerned.

The right to a fair hearing

10.25 Paragraph 70 of the 1990 Code of Audit Practice requires auditors to ensure that all persons who may be affected by exercise of their special powers under sections 19 and 20 of the 1982 Act have a fair and adequate opportunity to reply to any allegations or charges which are critical of or adverse to them.

10.26 In last line, for 'para.19' of Code of Audit Practice read 'para.76/1990'.

10.27 In line 10, for 'p.809' of *Wade,* read '(6th edn.), p.930'.

Right to know opposing case and evidence

10.29 In last line, for 'para.18' of Code of Audit Practice, read 'para.74/1990'.

10.32,n.17 For 'p.480' of *Wade,* read '(6th edn.), p.539'.

10.33 As to the investigatory or inquisitorial role of the auditor, see *dictum* of Woolf L.J. at 10.12-16, above.

In line 6, for 'para.18' of Code of Audit Practice, read 'para.74/ 1990'.

10.34A In *Public Disclosure Commission* v. *Isaacs,* [1988] 1 W.L.R. 1043, the Judicial Committee of the Privy Council held that the fundamental principle of the right to a fair hearing is that if a person may be adversely affected by an investigation and report he should be told the case against him and afforded a fair opportunity of answering it; but that this principle had no application to a complainant under the Bahamas Public Disclosure Act 1976 whose allegations concerning the Prime Minister's financial affairs had been investigated by the Public Disclosure Commission and dismissed without giving the complainant an opportunity of rebutting their findings. It was held that unless the Commission are minded to report that the complaint was frivolous or groundless, the claimant is not adversely affected by a decision that his case is not substantiated - he cannot be told the case made against him and afforded a fair opportunity of answering it because no case is made against him. It may be considered that this case has some application to the situation of an objector, though its application in a particular case would need to be considered with caution in the light of the circumstances of the case and judgments in other cases mentioned in the main text, 10.23-34.

Oral hearings

10.35   In line 4, for 'p.482' of *Wade*, read '(6th edn.), p.543'.

10.36   In place of the references to the Code of Audit Practice reference should be made to paragraph 75 of the 1990 Code, which states that there is no statutory requirement for an oral hearing, but that the auditor must consider whether justice or the public interest would best be served by giving those affected the opportunity of an oral hearing, and if so, whether that hearing should be in public.

10.36A   In the case of *Lloyd* v. *McMahon*, [1987] A.C. 625 (7.61A-C, above), exhaustive consideration was given by the Court of Appeal and the House of Lords to the question whether the auditor had acted unfairly in inviting representations in writing, rather than orally, from the councillors concerned. Some differences appeared in the judgments of the Court of Appeal. Lawton L.J. held that the auditor, while justified in inviting written representations in the first instance because oral hearings at that stage might have taken inordinate time, ought subsequently to have offered an oral hearing because the protestations of good faith in the councillors' written reply warranted an opportunity to establish their good faith orally. He held, however, that this omission was cured by the appeal to the Divisional Court, since that was a rehearing at which the councillors had every opportunity of giving any evidence they wished. Woolf and Dillon L.JJ. both agreed that the rehearing by the Divisional Court ruled out any question of the appellants having been prejudiced by the absence of an oral hearing before the auditor, and found it unnecessary to reach a conclusion on the fairness of the auditor's proceedings considered in isolation, though both expressed some reservations.

10.36B   The House of Lords unanimously rejected the view of Lawton L.J. in the Court of Appeal that the auditor should in fairness have offered an oral hearing. It was held that while there were circumstances where an oral hearing by an auditor would be essential or appropriate in the interests of fairness, this was not such a case, since:

(a)   the appellants had not asked for an oral hearing or indicated that they had any expectation of one. They had consistently presented a united defence and none had asked for an oral hearing to present an individual case (pp.696C, 706D, 714D);

(b)   the auditor's view was based on documentary evidence; no facts contradictory of or supplementary to the documents had appeared and no grounds could be discerned for the assertion that oral representations could have added to the written defence (pp.696E, 714B);

(c)   while an oral hearing would have enabled the appellants to reiterate the sincerity of their views, their sincerity could not justify unreasonable delay in performing a statutory duty (pp.696G, 708B, 714A).

Agreement was also expressed, *obiter*, with the view of the Court of Appeal that if there had been any unfairness in the auditor's procedure it would have been cured by the Divisional Court hearing (pp.697C, 708D, 717G).

10.36C   Some examples were given in their Lordships' speeches of circumstances in which an oral hearing by the auditor would be essential or desirable, as follows:

(a)   Where an objector states that he has personal knowledge of facts indicating wilful misconduct by a councillor - oral hearing essential in interests of fairness (p.696E).

(b)   Where a single individual is thought to have failed to bring a sum into account or by his wilful misconduct to have caused a loss or deficiency – a very appropriate practice to invite his explanation orally (p.706C).

(c)   If a councillor has wanted to put forward individual grounds in rebuttal of a charge
of wilful misconduct against himself and has asked to be heard orally - refusal clear
ground for complaint of unfairness (p.706E).

(d)   If an appellant had requested an oral hearing – desirable for the auditor to have
granted that request (p.714D).

10.37A   The question of oral hearings of objections was mentioned, *obiter*, in *Lloyd* v.
McMahon, by Woolf L.J., who said:

'The fact that the elector is required to attend to make an objection does not mean
that today the auditor is required to inquire into the objections in public or to hear
oral representations or evidence relating to the objection' (p.662F).

10.37B   The question arose again in *R.* v. *District Auditor, No.10 Audit District, ex parte Judge*,
(9.36B, above), where an objector having been granted leave to seek judicial review of
the auditor's dismissal of his objection without an oral hearing, the auditor applied to
set aside the leave. The auditor's application was granted mainly on the ground that the
objector should have raised the matter on appeal under section 19(4) of the 1982 Act
rather than by judicial review. But Rose J., at first instance, referred to the above-quoted
dictum of Woolf L.J. in *Lloyd* v. *McMahon* among the matters he had taken into account
(Transcript, Marten Walsh Cherer Ltd., pp.9C, 13D). The Court of Appeal, on appeal
by the objector, upheld the decisions and reasons of Rose J. and added that if the objector
had succeeded on technical grounds the court would have refused the appeal on
discretionary grounds; the court's only remedy on judicial review of this case would be
to require the auditor to reconsider the matter, and since he had given the objector full
opportunity to make his submissions in writing it was inconceivable that if he were to
hear the applicant in person he could come to any other conclusion (Transcript,
Association of Official Shorthandwriters Ltd., p.5).

10.40   In last line, for 'para.19' of Code of Audit Practice, read 'para.76/1990'.

10.44,n.25 For 'pp.485, 810 of *Wade*, read '(6th edn.), pp.546,931'.

Auditor's duties under section 19(1), etc.

10.45   Paragraph 70 of the 1990 Code of Audit Practice requires that in exercise of his
powers under sections 19 and 20 of the 1982 Act the auditor must ensure that all persons
who may be affected by such exercise have a fair and adequate opportunity to reply to
any allegations or charges which are critical of or adverse to them.

10.45,n.26   For 'p.504' of *Wade*, read '(6th edn.), p.570'.

10.47   In last line, for 'para.18' of Code of Audit Practice, read 'para.74/1990'.

10.47,n.27   For 'p.482' of *Wade*, read '(6th edn.), p.543'.

III   EVIDENCE

Rules of evidence

10.49-50,n.28 For 'p.806' of *Wade*, read '(6th edn.), p.926, n.76'.

Admissions and confessions

10.55   The law relating to the admissibility of confessions in criminal proceedings is now
governed by the Police and Criminal Evidence Act 1984. Section 76 provides that a
confession will be excluded from criminal proceedings if it is represented to the court

that it was obtained by oppression or in consequence of anything said or done which was likely to render the confession unreliable, unless the prosecution proves beyond reasonable doubt that the confession was not obtained in that way. Section 78 gives a criminal court a discretion to exclude prosecution evidence if it considers, because of the circumstances in which the evidence was obtained or otherwise, that the evidence would have such an adverse effect on the fairness of the proceedings that it should not be admitted.

10.56 The Judges' Rules have been superseded by Code of Practice C issued by the Secretary of State under section 66(b) of the 1984 Act in connection with the detention, treatment, questioning and identification of persons by police officers. This Code covers generally the ground formerly in the Judges' Rules and also makes additional provision relating to interrogation procedure. It provides that 'A person whom there are grounds to suspect of an offence must be cautioned before any questions about it... are put to him for the purpose of obtaining evidence which may be given to a court in a prosecution' (para.10.1); and that the caution is to be in the terms 'You do not have to say anything unless you wish to do so, but what you say may be given in evidence'; minor deviations are permissible (para.10.4). Section 67(9) of the 1984 Act provides that 'Persons other than police officers who are charged with the duty of investigating offences or charging offenders shall in the discharge of that duty have regard to any relevant provision of such a code'. Section 67(11) provides that the code shall be admissible in evidence in criminal and civil proceedings and shall be taken into account if considered relevant to questions arising in the proceedings.

10.57 It does not appear that the conclusions in this paragraph of the main text are affected by the changes noted above. The investigators covered by section 67(9) are the same as those referred to in Rule VI of the Judges' Rules and likewise do not appear to include local government auditors (or health service auditors, to whom the last sentence of the main text equally applies). There was nothing in the Judges' Rules corresponding to section 67(11) of the 1984 Act, but it does not appear that this effects any change of substance; it has always been possible in civil proceedings to affect the weight of an admission (though not to render it inadmissible) by evidence of surrounding irregularity, for example by showing that it was made in consequence of threats or inducements (Cross, *Evidence*, 7th edn., p.580).

10.58 It does not appear that the conclusions in this paragraph are changed by the replacement of the Judges' Rules by the provisions of the Police and Criminal Evidence Act 1984 and the Code made under section 66 thereof.

Burden/standard of proof

10.60,n.36 For 'p.97' of *Cross*, read '(7th edn.), p.123'.

10.60,n.37 For '13th' edn., of *Phipson*, read '14th'.

10.62 The quotation from the Code of Audit Practice is repeated in substance in paragraph 76 of the 1990 Code.

10.63 In *Lloyd* v. *McMahon*, [1987] A.C. 625, Lawton L.J. said 'As to the burden of proof, although a section 20 enquiry is not a criminal proceeding, nevertheless, following what Denning L.J. said in *Hornal* v. *Neuberger Products Ltd.*, it should take a lot of evidence to tip the balance in favour of a positive finding because the accusation is serious and the consequences grave' (p.647A). Applying that criterion he held that the appellant councillors were guilty of wilful misconduct in failing to levy a rate in due time (as did the other members of the Court of Appeal). On this issue the House of Lords agreed that the courts below had applied the right test and found it unnecessary to add to their reasoning (pp.697H, 702C).

10.63,n.38   For '5th edn., Ch.V' of *Cross*, read '7th edn., Ch.III,Sect.3'.

10.64,n.39   For '5th edn., pp.457-8' of *Cross,* read '7th edn., pp.102-3'.

IV   PROCEDURE

10.66,68   For references to paragraphs 14 and 15 to 20 of the Code of Audit Practice, read paragraphs 70 and 71 to 77 of the 1990 Code.

As to the delegation of the hearing of objections, see 2.71, above.

10.67   The 1990 Code of Audit Practice requires that notice of an objection should be given to any persons who may be affected by a decision upon the objection in order that they may have an opportunity to deal with any matter adverse to them (para.73), and that where there is an oral hearing all persons concerned should be given due notice to be present or represented at the hearing to deal with any matters affecting them (para.75).

10.74   In last line, for 'App., para.9' of Code of Audit Practice, read 'para.49/1990'.

V   ADMISSION OF THE PUBLIC

Oral hearings of objections

10.80-3   The first part of paragraph 19 of the 1983 Code of Audit Practice, as reproduced in paragraph 10.80 of the main text, was omitted from the Codes published in 1988 and 1990. On the subject of the admission of the public to the oral hearing of objections the 1990 Code requires only that 'The auditor must consider whether justice or the public interest would be best served by giving those affected the opportunity of an oral hearing, and if so, whether that hearing should be in public' (para.75); and that 'At such a hearing... if it becomes apparent that injustices may be caused by allegations made without due notice, the public should be excluded' (para.76). The omission of the first sentence of paragraph 19 of the 1983 Code meets the points made at paragraphs 10.81-3, main text.

APPENDIX A

STATUTES

A.1. LOCAL GOVERNMENT FINANCE ACT 1982

PART III
ACCOUNTS AND AUDIT
The Audit Commission

Establishment of Audit Commission

11.–(1) For the purposes of this Part of this Act there shall be a body to be known as the Audit Commission for Local Authorities [and the National Health Service] in England and Wales.

(2) The Commission shall consist of not less than [fifteen] nor more than [twenty] members appointed by the Secretary of State after consultation with [such organisations and other bodies as appear to him to be appropriate].

(3) The Secretary of State shall, after the like consultation, appoint one of the members to be chairman and another to be deputy chairman.

(4) Schedule 3 to this Act shall have effect with respect to the Commission.

AMENDMENTS

The words in square brackets in subss.(1) and (2) were inserted or substituted by the National Health Service and Community Care Act 1990, s.20, Sch.4, para.1.

Audit of Accounts

Accounts subject to audit

12.–(1) All accounts to which this section applies shall be made up yearly to 31st March or such other date as the Secretary of State may generally or in any special case direct and shall be audited in accordance with this Part of this Act by an auditor or auditors appointed by the Commission.

(2) This section applies to all accounts of–

(a) a local authority;

[(aa) a joint authority;]

(ab) [...]

(b) a parish meeting of a parish not having a separate parish council;

(c) a committee of a local authority, including a joint committee of two or more such authorities;

(d) the Council of the Isles of Scilly;

(e) any charter trustees constituted under section 246 of the Local Government Act 1972;

[(ea) a body specified in section 98(1) of the National Health Service Act 1977;]

(f) a port health authority;

[(ff) the Broads Authority]

(g) a combined police authority;

(h) a fire authority constituted by a combination scheme;

(i) a licensing planning committee;

(j) an internal drainage board;

(k) a children's regional planning committee; and

(l) a [probation committee] [except the committee for the inner London area].

[(3) This section also applies to-

(a) the accounts of the collection fund of the Common Council and the accounts of the City fund; and

(b) the accounts relating to the superannuation fund established and administered by the Common Council under the Local Government Superannuation Regulations 1974 as amended by the Local Government Superannuation (City of London) Regulations 1977;

and any reference in this Part of this Act to the accounts of a body shall be construed, in relation to the Common Council, as a reference to the accounts mentioned in paragraphs (a) and (b) above.]

[(3A) This section also applies to the accounts of the members of a recognised fund-holding practice so far as they relate to allotted sums paid to them, and subject to subsection (3B) and section 16(1A) below, any reference in this Part of this Act to the accounts of a body shall be construed, in relation to the members of a fund-holding practice, as a reference to such of their accounts as relate to allotted sums so paid.

(3B) In such circumstances and to such extent as regulations made by the Secretary of State so provide, this Part of this Act shall not apply to the accounts for any year of the members of a recognised fund-holding practice if those accounts are submitted to a Family Health Services Authority and summarised in that Authority's accounts.

(3C) In subsection (3A) above "allotted sums" has the same meaning as in section 15 of the National Health Service and Community Care Act 1990.]

(4) References in any statutory provision or document to district audit, to audit by a district auditor, to audit in accordance with Part VIII of the Local Government Act 1972 or to professional audit shall be construed, in relation to the accounts of a local authority or other public body, as references to audit as mentioned in subsection (1) above.

[(5) Any reference in this Part of this Act to a health service body is a reference to a body specified in section 98(1) of the National Health Service Act 1977 or to the members of a recognised fund-holding practice as mentioned in subsection (3A) above.]

AMENDMENTS

In subs.(2) the words in, or formerly in, square brackets were inserted or substituted by s.72, Local Government Act 1985 (paras.(aa) and (ab)); s.17, Norfolk and Suffolk Broads Act 1988 (para.(ff); s.65(1), Criminal Justice Act 1982 and para.8, Sch.11, Criminal Justice Act 1988 (para.(1)); para.2(1), Sch.4, National Health Service and Community Care Act 1990 (para.(ea)).

The Education Reform Act 1988, s.237 and Sch.13, Pt.I, repealed subs.2(ab) with effect from 1 April 1990 (s.236(5)).

Subs.(3) was substituted by the Local Government Finance Act 1988, s.137 and Sch.12, para.3.

Subss.(3A) to (3C) and (5) were inserted by the National Health Service and Community Care Act 1990, s.20, Sch.4, para.2(2), (3).

Appointment of auditors

13.–(1) An auditor appointed by the Commission to audit the accounts of any body whose accounts are required to be audited in accordance with this Part of this Act may be an officer of the Commission, an individual who is not such an officer or a firm of such individuals.

(2) Where two or more auditors are appointed in relation to the accounts of any body, some but not others may be officers of the Commission and they may be appointed to act jointly, to act separately in relation to different parts of the accounts or to discharge different functions in relation to the audit.

(3) Before appointing any auditor or auditors to audit the accounts of any body [other than a health service body] the Commission shall consult that body.

(4) For the purpose of assisting the Commission in deciding on the appointment of an auditor or auditors in relation to the accounts of any body [other than a health service body] the Commission may require that body to make available for inspection by or on behalf of the Commission such documents relating to any accounts of the body as the Commission may reasonably require for that purpose.

(5) A person shall not be appointed by the Commission as an auditor unless he is a member of one or more of the bodies mentioned in subsection (6) below or has such other qualifications as may be approved for the purposes of this section by the Secretary of State [or is a person for the time being approved by the Secretary of State, acting on the recommendation of the Commission]; and a firm shall not be so appointed unless each of its members is a member of one or more of those bodies.

[(5A) The Secretary of State shall not approve any person for the purposes of subsection (5) above after 31st March 1996 but, subject to the withdrawal of his approval after that date, any person who is so approved immediately before that date shall continue to be so approved after that date.]

(6) The bodies referred to in subsection (5) above are–

  (a) the Institute of Chartered Accountants in England and Wales;

  (b) the Institute of Chartered Accountants of Scotland;

  (c) the Association of Certified Accountants;

  (d) the Chartered Institute of Public Finance and Accountancy;

  (e) the Institute of Chartered Accountants in Ireland; and

  (f) any other body of accountants established in the United Kingdom and for the time being approved by the Secretary of State for the purposes of this section.

(7) The appointment by the Commission of an auditor who is not an officer of the Commission shall be on such terms and for such period as the Commission may determine.

(8) Arrangements may be approved by the Commission, either generally or in any particular case, for a person or persons to assist an auditor appointed by the Commission by carrying out such of his functions under this Part of this Act as may be specified in the arrangements; and references in the following provisions of this Part of this Act to an auditor include, in relation to any function of an auditor, a reference to any person carrying out that function under arrangements approved under this subsection.

(9) Subsection (8) above applies whether or not the auditor is an officer of the Commission.

AMENDMENTS

Subs.(5A) and the words in square brackets in subss.(3), (4) and (5) were inserted by the National Health Service and Community Care Act 1990, s.20, Sch.4, para.3.

Code of Audit Practice

14.–(1) The Commission shall prepare, and keep under review, a code of audit practice prescribing the way in which auditors are to carry out their functions under this Part of this Act [and a different code may be prepared with respect to the audit of the accounts of health service bodies as compared with the code applicable to the accounts of other bodies.]

(2) The code shall embody what appears to the Commission to be the best professional practice with respect to the standards, procedures and techniques to be adopted by auditors.

(3) The code shall not come into force until approved by a resolution of each House of Parliament, and its continuation in force shall be subject to its being so approved at intervals of not more than five years.

(4) Subsection (3) above shall not preclude alterations to the code being made by the Commission in the intervals between its being approved as aforesaid.

(5) The Commission shall send copies of the code and of any alterations made to the code to the Secretary of State who shall lay them before Parliament; and the Commission shall from time to time publish the code as for the time being in force.

(6) Before preparing the code or making any alteration in it the Commission shall consult such associations of local authorities as appear to it to be concerned and such bodies of accountants as appear to it to be appropriate.

[(7) In the application of subsection (6) above to a code which relates to the accounts of health service bodies,-

(a) if the code relates only to those accounts, the reference to associations of local authorities shall be construed as a reference to organisations connected with the health service, within the meaning of the National Health Service Act 1977; and

(b) if the code relates also to the accounts of other bodies, that reference shall be construed as including a reference to such organisations.]

AMENDMENTS

Subs.(7) and the words in square brackets in subs.(1) were inserted by the National Health Service and Community Care Act 1990, s.20, Sch.4, para.4.

General duties of auditors

15.–(1) In auditing any accounts required to be audited in accordance with this Part of this Act, an auditor shall by examination of the accounts and otherwise satisfy himself-

(a) that the accounts are prepared in accordance with regulations made under section 23 below [or, in the case of a health service body, directions under subsection (2) or subsection (2B) of section 98 of the National Health Service Act 1977] and comply with the requirements of all other statutory provisions applicable to the accounts;

(b) that proper practices have been observed in the compilation of the accounts; and

(c) that the body whose accounts are being audited has made proper arrangements for securing economy, efficiency and effectiveness in its use of resources.

(2) The auditor shall comply with the code of audit practice as for the time being in force.

(3) The auditor shall consider whether, in the public interest, he should make a report on any matter coming to his notice in the course of the audit in order that it may be considered by the body concerned or brought to the attention of the public, and shall consider whether the public interest requires any such matter to be made the subject of an immediate report rather than of a report to be made at the conclusion of the audit.

AMENDMENT

The words in square brackets in subs.(1) were inserted by the National Health Service and Community Care Act 1990, s.20, Sch.4, para.5.

Auditor's right to obtain documents and information

16.–(1) An auditor shall have a right of access at all reasonable times to all such documents relating to a body whose accounts are required to be audited in accordance with this Part of this Act as appear to him necessary [for the purposes of his functions under this Act] and shall be entitled to require from any person holding or accountable for any such document such information and explanation as he thinks necessary for those purposes and, if he thinks it necessary, to require any such person to attend before him in person to give the information or explanation or to produce any such document.

[(1A) In the case of a recognised fund-holding practice the reference in subsection (1) above to documents includes a reference to documents relating to all the accounts and records of the members of the practice, whether or not relating to the allotted sum, within the meaning of that section.]

(2) Without prejudice to subsection (1) above, the auditor shall be entitled to require any officer or member of a body whose accounts are required to be audited in accordance with this Part of this Act to give him such information or explanation as he thinks necessary [for the purposes of his functions under this Act] and, if he thinks it necessary, to require any such officer or member to attend before him in person to give the information or explanation.

(3) Without prejudice to subsections (1) and (2) above, every body whose accounts are required to be audited in accordance with this Part of this Act shall provide the auditor with every facility and all information which he may reasonably require [for the purposes of his functions under this Act].

(4) Any person who without reasonable excuse fails to comply with any requirement of an auditor under subsection (1) or (2) above shall be liable on summary conviction to a fine not exceeding [level 3 on the standard scale] and to an additional fine not exceeding £20 for each day on which the offence continues after conviction thereof.

(5) Any expenses incurred by an auditor in connection with proceedings for an offence under subsection (4) above alleged to have been committed in relation to the audit of the accounts of any body shall, so far as not recovered from any other source, be recoverable from that body.

AMENDMENTS

The words in square brackets in subss.(1), (2) and (3) were substituted by the Local Government Act 1988, s.30(2).

Subs.(1A) was inserted by the National Health Service and Community Care Act 1990, s.20, Sch.4, para.6.

The words in square brackets in subs.(4) were substituted by the Criminal Justice Act 1982, ss.38 and 46. The fine on level 3 of the standard scale is currently £400 (Criminal Penalties etc. (Increase) Order 1984, S.I. 1984/447).

Public inspection of accounts and right of challenge

17.–(1) At each audit by an auditor under this Part of this Act [other than the audit of the accounts of a health service body] any persons interested may inspect the accounts to be audited and all books, deeds, contracts, bills, vouchers and receipts relating to them and make copies of all or any part of the accounts and those other documents.

(2) At the request of a local government elector for any area to which those accounts relate, the auditor shall give the elector, or any representative of his, an opportunity to question the auditor about the accounts.

(3) Subject to subsection (4) below, any local government elector for any area to which those accounts relate, or any representative of his, may attend before the auditor and make objections-

(a) as to any matter in respect of which the auditor could take action under section 19 or 20 below; or

(b) as to any other matter in respect of which the auditor could make a report under section 15(3) above.

(4) No objection may be made under subsection (3) above by or on behalf of a local government elector unless the auditor has previously received written notice of the proposed objection and of the grounds on which it is to be made.

(5) Where an elector sends a notice to an auditor for the purposes of subsection (4) above he shall at the same time send a copy of the notice to the body whose accounts are the subject of the audit.

AMENDMENT

The words in square brackets in subs.(1) were inserted by the National Health Service and Community Care Act 1990, s.20, Sch.4, para.7.

Auditor's reports

18.–(1) When an auditor has concluded his audit of the accounts of any body under this Part of this Act-

(a) a certificate that he has completed the audit in accordance with this Part of this Act; and

(b) his opinion on the relevant statement of accounts prepared pursuant to regulations under section 23 below (or, where no such statement is required to be prepared, on the accounts),

shall, subject to subsection (2) below, be entered by him on the statement (or, as the case may be, on the accounts).

(2) Where an auditor makes a report to the body concerned under section 15(3) above at the conclusion of the audit, the certificate and opinion referred to in subsection (1) above may be included by him in that report.

(3) Any report under section 15(3) above shall be sent by the auditor to the body concerned or, in the case of a parish meeting, to the chairman, and (except in the case of an immediate report) shall be so sent not later than fourteen days after the conclusion

of the audit, and that body shall take the report into consideration as soon as practicable after they have received it.

(4) A copy of any such report shall be sent by the auditor to the Commission [and, in the case of a health service body, to the Secretary of State] forthwith, if the report is an immediate report, and otherwise not later than fourteen days after the conclusion of the audit.

(5) The agenda supplied to the members of a body for the meeting of the body at which they take into consideration a report of an auditor sent to them under subsection (3) above shall be accompanied by that report, and the report shall not be excluded-

[(a) from the matter supplied for the benefit of any newspaper under section 1(4)(b) of the Public Bodies (Admission to Meetings) Act 1960 (supply of agenda of meetings and related documents to newspapers) [or under section 100B(7) of the 1972 Act (which makes similar provision); or

(b) from the documents open to inspection by members of the public under section 100B (1) of the 1972 Act (agenda and reports open to the public before a meeting);

and Part VA of the 1972 Act shall have effect in relation to the report as if in section 100C(1)(d) of that Act (by virtue of which only so much of a report as relates to proceedings open to the public is open to public inspection after the meeting) the words 'so much of' and from 'as relates' onwards were omitted.

(6) In subsection (5) above, 'the 1972 Act' means the Local Government Act 1972].

AMENDMENTS

The words in square brackets in subs.(4) were inserted by the National Health Service and Community Care Act 1990, s.20, Sch.4, para.8.

The words in square brackets in subss.(5) and (6) were inserted by the Local Government (Access to Information) Act 1985, Sch.2, para.7.

[Additional publicity for auditors' immediate reports

18A.–(1) As from the time when, by virtue of section 18(3) above, an immediate report made under section 15(3) above is received by a body or by the chairman of a parish meeting, any member of the public shall be entitled-

(a) to inspect the report at all reasonable times and without payment and to make a copy of it, or of any part of it, and

(b) to require the body or chairman to supply to him a copy of the report, or of any part of it, on payment of a reasonable sum.

(2) When such a report is so received by a body or by the chairman of a parish meeting, the body or chairman shall forthwith publish in one or more local newspapers circulating in the area of the body or meeting a notice which-

(a) identifies the subject-matter of the report, and

(b) states that any member of the public–
(i) may inspect the report, and
(ii) may make a copy of it, or of any part of it,
between such times and at such place or places as are specified in the notice;

and, where the report is so received by a body, the body shall in addition forthwith supply a copy of the report to every member of the body.

(3) Any person having the custody of an immediate report who-

(a) obstructs a person in the exercise of any right conferred by subsection (1)(a) above, or

(b) refuses to supply a copy of the report, or (as the case may be) of any part of it, to a person entitled to such a copy by virtue of subsection (1)(b) above,

shall be liable on summary conviction to a fine not exceeding level 3 on the standard scale.

(4) Any person who fails to comply with any requirement of subsection (2) above shall be liable on summary conviction to a fine not exceeding level 3 on the standard scale.

(5) An auditor who has sent an immediate report to a body or to the chairman of a parish meeting under section 18(3) above-

(a) may notify any person he thinks fit of the fact that he has made such a report, and

(b) may supply a copy of the report, or of any part of it, to any person he thinks fit.

(6) Nothing in this section applies in relation to a health service body.

(7) Nothing in this section is to be construed as affecting the operation of section 18(5) above.]

AMENDMENT

Section 18A was inserted by the Local Government Finance (Publicity for Auditors' Reports) Act 1991, s.1(2).

Declaration that item of account is unlawful

19.–(1) Where it appears to the auditor carrying out the audit of any accounts under this Part of this Act [other than the audit of the accounts of a health service body] that any item of account is contrary to law he may apply to the court for a declaration that the item is contrary to law except where it is sanctioned by the Secretary of State.

(2) On an application under this section the court may make or refuse to make the declaration asked for, and where the court makes that declaration, then, subject to subsection (3) below, it may also-

(a) order that any person responsible for incurring or authorising any expenditure declared unlawful shall repay it in whole or in part to the body in question and, where two or more persons are found to be responsible, that they shall be jointly and severally liable to repay it as aforesaid;

(b) if any such expenditure exceeds £2,000 and the person responsible for incurring or authorising it is, or was at the time of his conduct in question, a member of a local authority, order him to be disqualified for being a member of a local authority for a specified period; and

(c) order rectification of the accounts.

(3) The court shall not make an order under subsection (2)(a) or (b) above if the court is satisfied that the person responsible for incurring or authorising any such expenditure acted reasonably or in the belief that the expenditure was authorised by law, and in any other case shall have regard to all the circumstances, including that person's means and ability to repay that expenditure or any part of it.

(4) Any person who has made an objection under section 17(3)(a) above and is aggrieved by a decision of an auditor not to apply for a declaration under this section may-

(a) not later than six weeks after he has been notified of the decision, require the auditor to state in writing the reasons for his decision; and

(b) appeal against the decision to the court,

and on any such appeal the court shall have the like powers in relation to the item of account to which the objection relates as if the auditor had applied for the declaration.

(5) On an application or appeal under this section relating to the accounts of a body, the court may make such order as the court thinks fit for the payment by that body of expenses incurred in connection with the application or appeal by the auditor or the person to whom the application or appeal relates or by whom the appeal is brought, as the case may be.

(6) [The High Court and the county courts shall have jurisdiction for the purposes of this section].

(7) In this section "local authority" includes [...] the Common Council and the Council of the Isles of Scilly.

AMENDMENTS

The words in square brackets in subs.(1) were inserted by the National Health Service and Community Care Act 1990, s.20, Sch.4, para.9.

The words omitted from the square brackets in subs.(7) were inserted by the Local Government Reorganisation (Miscellaneous Provision) (No.7) Order 1986, S.I. 1986/2293, art.2, and repealed from 1 April 1990 by the Education Reform Act 1988, ss.236(5), 237, Sch.13, Pt.I.

Subs.(6) was substituted by the High Court and County Courts Jurisdiction Order 1991 (S.I. 1991/724), art.2(8) and Sch., Pt.I.

Recovery of amount not accounted for etc.

20.–(1) Where it appears to the auditor carrying out the audit of any accounts under this Part of this Act [other than the audit of the accounts of a health service body]-

- (a) that any person has failed to bring into account any sum which should have been so included and that the failure has not been sanctioned by the Secretary of State; or

- (b) that a loss has been incurred or deficiency caused by the wilful misconduct of any person,

he shall certify that the sum or, as the case may be, the amount of the loss or the deficiency is due from that person and, subject to subsections (3) and (5) below, both he and the body in question (or, in the case of a parish meeting, the chairman of the meeting) may recover that sum or amount for the benefit of that body; and if the auditor certifies under this section that any sum or amount is due from two or more persons, they shall be jointly and severally liable for that sum or amount.

(2) Any person who-

- (a) has made an objection under section 17(3)(a) above and is aggrieved by a decision of an auditor not to certify under this section that a sum or amount is due from another person; or

- (b) is aggrieved by a decision of an auditor to certify under this section that a sum or amount is due from him,

may not later than six weeks after he has been notified of the decision require the auditor to state in writing the reasons for his decision.

(3) Any such person who is aggrieved by such a decision may appeal against the decision to the court and-

- (a) in the case of a decision to certify that any sum or amount is due from any person, the court may confirm, vary or quash the decision and give any certificate which the auditor could have given;

(b) in the case of a decision not to certify that any sum or amount is due from any person, the court may confirm the decision or quash it and give any certificate which the auditor could have given;

and any certificate given under this subsection shall be treated for the purposes of subsection (1) above and the following provisions of this section as if it had been given by the auditor under subsection (1) above.

(4) If a certificate under this section relates to a loss or deficiency caused by the wilful misconduct of a person who is, or was at the time of such misconduct, a member of a local authority and the amount certified to be due from him exceeds £2,000, that person shall be disqualified for being a member of a local authority for the period of five years beginning on the ordinary date on which the period allowed for bringing an appeal against a decision to give the certificate expires or, if such an appeal is brought, the date on which the appeal is finally disposed of or abandoned or fails for non-prosecution.

(5) A sum or other amount certified under this section to be due from any person shall be payable within fourteen days after the date of the issue of the certificate or, if an appeal is brought, within fourteen days after the appeal is finally disposed of or abandoned or fails for non-prosecution.

(6) In any proceedings for the recovery of any sum or amount due from any person under this section a certificate signed by an auditor appointed by the Commission stating that that sum or amount is due from a person specified in the certificate to a body so specified shall be conclusive evidence of that fact; and any certificate purporting to be so signed shall be taken to have been so signed unless the contrary is proved.

(7) On an appeal under this section relating to the accounts of a body, the court may make such order as the court thinks fit for the payment by that body of expenses incurred in connection with the appeal by the auditor or the person to whom the appeal relates or by whom the appeal is brought, as the case may be.

(8) Any expenses incurred by an auditor in recovering a sum or other amount certified under this section to be due in connection with the accounts of a body shall, so far as not recovered from any other source, be recoverable from that body unless the court otherwise directs.

(9) [The High Court and the county courts shall have jurisdiction for the purposes of this section].

(10) In this section "local authority" includes [...] the Common Council and the Council of the Isles of Scilly.

AMENDMENTS

The words in square brackets in subs.(1) were inserted by the National Health Service and Community Care Act 1990, s.20, Sch.4, para.10.

The words omitted from the square brackets in subs.(10) were inserted by the Local Government Reorganisation (Miscellaneous Provision) (No.7) Order 1986, S.I. 1986/2293, art.2, and repealed from 1 April 1990 by the Education Reform Act 1988, ss.236(5), 237, Sch.13, Pt.I.

Subs.(9) was substituted by the High Court and County Courts Jurisdiction Order 1991 (S.I. 1991/724), art.2(8) and Sch., Pt.I.

Fees for audit

21.–(1) The Commission shall prescribe a scale or scales of fees in respect of the audit of accounts which are required to be audited in accordance with this Part of this Act.

(2) Before prescribing any scale of fees under subsection (1) above the Commission shall consult such associations of local authorities as appear to it to be concerned and such bodies of accountants as appear to it to be appropriate.

[(2A) In the application of subsection (2) above to the audit of the accounts of a health service body, the reference to associations of local authorities shall be construed as a reference to organisations connected with the health service.]

(3) A body whose accounts are audited in accordance with this Part of this Act shall, subject to subsection (4) below, pay to the Commission the fee applicable to the audit in accordance with the appropriate scale.

(4) If it appears to the Commission that the work involved in a particular audit was substantially more or less than that envisaged by the appropriate scale, the Commission may charge a fee which is larger or smaller than that referred to in subsection (3) above.

(5) For the purpose of determining the fee payable for an audit, a body whose accounts are being audited (or, in the case of the accounts of a parish meeting, the chairman of the meeting) shall complete a statement containing such information as the Commission may require and submit it to the auditor who shall send it to the Commission on the conclusion of the audit with a certificate that the statement is correct to the best of his knowledge and belief; and, in addition, the body shall furnish the Commission with such further information as it may at any time require for the said purpose.

(6) The fee payable for an audit shall be the same whether the audit is carried out by an auditor who is an officer of the Commission or by an auditor who is not such an officer.

(7) If the Secretary of State considers it necessary or desirable to do so, he may by regulations prescribe a scale or scales of fees to have effect, for such period as is specified in the regulations, in place of any scale or scales prescribed by the Commission and, if he does so, references in subsections (3) and (4) above to the appropriate scale shall, as respects that period, be construed as references to the appropriate scale prescribed by the Secretary of State.

AMENDMENT

Subs. (2A) was inserted by the National Health Service and Community Care Act 1990, s.20, Sch.4, para.11.

Extraordinary audit

22.–(1) [Subject to subsection (4A) below] the Commission may direct an auditor or auditors appointed by it to hold an extraordinary audit of the accounts of any body whose accounts are required to be audited in accordance with this Part of this Act if-

    (a) an application in that behalf is made by a local government elector for the area of that body; or

    (b) it appears to the Commission to be desirable to do so in consequence of a report made under this Part of this Act by an auditor or for any other reason.

(2) If it appears to the Secretary of State that it is desirable in the public interest that there should be an extraordinary audit of the accounts of any such body as aforesaid he may require the Commission to direct such an audit by an auditor or auditors appointed by it.

(3) [Subject to subsection (4A) below] the provisions of sections 13 and 15 to 20 above, except subsections (1) and (2) of section 17, shall apply to an extraordinary audit under this section as they apply to an ordinary audit under this Part of this Act.

(4) An extraordinary audit under this section may be held after three clear days notice in writing given to the body whose accounts are to be audited or, in the case of the accounts of a parish meeting, to the chairman of the meeting.

[(4A) Subsection (1)(a) above does not apply in relation to the accounts of a health service body; and in the application of subsection (3) above to an extraordinary audit of any such accounts for the words "15 to 20 above, except subsections (1) and (2) of section 17" there shall be substituted "15, 16, and 18 above".]

(5) The expenditure incurred in holding an extraordinary audit of the accounts of any body shall be defrayed in the first instance by the Commission but it may, if it thinks fit, recover the whole or any proportion of that expenditure from that body.

AMENDMENTS

Subs.(4A), and the words in square brackets in subss.(1) and (3), were inserted by the National Health Service and Community Care Act 1990, s.20, Sch.4, para.12.

Regulations as to accounts

23.–(1) The Secretary of State may by regulations applying to bodies whose accounts are required to be audited in accordance with this Part of this Act [other than health service bodies] make provision with respect to-

(a) the keeping of accounts;

(b) the form, preparation and certification of accounts and of statements of accounts;

(c) the deposit of the accounts of any body at the offices of the body or at any other place;

(d) the publication of information relating to accounts and the publication of statements of accounts;

(e) the exercise of any rights of inspection or objection conferred by section 17 above or section 24 below and the steps to be taken by any body for informing local government electors for the area of that body of those rights.

(2) Regulations under this section may make different provision in relation to bodies of different descriptions.

(3) Any person who without reasonable excuse contravenes any provision of regulations under this section, the contravention of which is declared by the regulations to be an offence, shall be liable on summary conviction to a fine not exceeding [level 3 on the standard scale].

(4) Any expenses incurred by an auditor in connection with proceedings in respect of an offence under subsection (3) above alleged to have been committed in relation to the accounts of any body shall, so far as not recovered from any other source, be recoverable from that body.

AMENDMENTS

The words in square brackets in subs.(1) were inserted by the National Health Service and Community Care Act 1990, s.20, Sch.4, para.13.

The words in square brackets in subs.(3) were substituted by the Criminal Justice Act 1982, ss.38 and 46. The fine on level 3 of the standard scale is currently £400 (Criminal Penalties etc (Increase) Order 1984, S.I. 1984/447).

Right to inspect statements of accounts and auditor's reports

24.–(1) Any local government elector for the area of a body whose accounts are required to be audited in accordance with this Part of this Act [other than a health service body] shall be entitled-

  (a) to inspect and make copies of any statement of accounts prepared by the body pursuant to regulations under section 23 above and any report made to the body by an auditor [other than an immediate report]; and

  (b) to require copies of any such statement or report to be delivered to him on payment of a reasonable sum for each copy.

(2) Any document which a person is entitled to inspect under this section may be inspected by him at all reasonable times and without payment.

(3) Any person having the custody of any such document who-

  (a) obstructs a person in the exercise of any right under this section to inspect or make copies of the document; or

  (b) refuses to give copies of the document to a person entitled under this section to obtain them,

shall be liable on summary conviction to a fine not exceeding [level 3 on the standard scale].

(4) References in this section to copies of a document include references to copies of any part of it.

AMENDMENTS

The words in square brackets in subs.(1) were inserted by the National Health Service and Community Care Act 1990, s.20, Sch.4, para.14, and (in para.(a)) by the Local Government Finance (Publicity for Auditors' Reports) Act 1991, s.1(3).

The words in square brackets in subs.(3) were substituted by the Criminal Justice Act 1982, ss.38 and 46. The fine on level 3 of the standard scale is currently £400 (Criminal Penalties etc (Increase) Order 1984, S.I. 1984/447).

Audit of accounts of officers

25.–(1) Where an officer of a body whose accounts are required to be audited in accordance with this Part of this Act receives any money or other property on behalf of that body or receives any money or other property for which he ought to account to that body the accounts of the officer shall be audited by the auditor of the accounts of that body and sections 12(1) and 15 to 24 above shall with the necessary modifications apply accordingly to the accounts and audit.

  [(2) In the application of subsection (1) above to an officer of a health service body for the words "15 to 24" there shall be substituted "15, 16, 18, 21 and 22".]

AMENDMENT

Subs.(2) was inserted by the National Health Service and Community Care Act 1990, s.20, Sch.4, para.15.

[Power of auditor to issue prohibition order

25A.–(1) The person who is for the time being the auditor in relation to the accounts of any body whose accounts are required to be audited in accordance with this Part of this Act [other than a health service body] may issue an order under this section (in this Part referred to as a "prohibition order") if he has reason to believe that the body or any officer of the body-

(a) is about to make or has made a decision which involves or would involve the body incurring expenditure which is unlawful; or

(b) is about to take or has taken a course of action which, if pursued to its conclusion, would be unlawful and likely to cause a loss or deficiency; or

(c) is about to enter an item of account, the entry of which is unlawful;

and for the purposes of this section and section 25B below, the actions of a committee or sub-committee of the body or of any other person (not being an officer) authorised to act on behalf of the body shall be treated as the actions of the body itself.

(2) A prohibition order is one–

(a) which is addressed to the body or officer concerned;

(b) which specifies the paragraph of subsection (1) above which is relevant and the decision, course of action or item of account to which the order relates;

(c) which specifies the date on which (subject to subsection (5) below) the order is to take effect, being a date not earlier than the date of service of a copy of the order in accordance with paragraph (a) or, as the case may be, paragraphs (a) and (b) of subsection (4) below; and

(d) which requires the body or officer concerned to desist from making or implementing the decision, taking or continuing to take the course of action, or, as the case may be, entering the item of account in question.

(3) Where two or more auditors are appointed in relation to the accounts of any body, the power to issue a prohibition order may be exercised by the auditors acting jointly or by such one of them as they may determine; and, in relation to such an order, any reference in subsections (4) and (5) below to the auditor is a reference to the auditor or auditors by whom the order is issued.

(4) A copy of a prohibition order–

(a) shall be served on the body to which, or to an officer of which, it is addressed; and

(b) in the case of an order addressed to an officer, shall also be served on him; and

(c) may be served on such other person or persons as appears to the auditor to be appropriate.

(5) A prohibition order shall not have effect unless, not later than the end of the period of seven days beginning on the date of service referred to in subsection (2)(c) above, the auditor serves on the body concerned and on any officer on whom a copy of the order was served under subsection (4)(b) above, a statement of the auditor's reasons for the belief referred to in subsection (1) above.

(6) Any copy of an order or statement which under this section is to be served on an officer of a body shall be served on him by addressing it to him and by delivering it to him or leaving it at, or sending it by post to, the office at which he is employed.

(7) A prohibition order may at any time be revoked (but not varied) by the person who is for the time being the auditor in relation to the accounts of the body to which or to an officer of which the order was addressed.]

AMENDMENTS

Section 25A was inserted by the Local Government Act 1988, s.30(1) and Sch.4.

The words in square brackets in subs.(1) were inserted by the National Health Service and Community Care Act 1990, s.20, Sch.4, para.16.

[Restriction on power to issue prohibition order

25AA.–(1) In a case where-

    (a) a report is made under section 114(2) of the Local Government Finance Act 1988 (the 1988 Act), and

    (b) copies of the report are sent in accordance with section 114(4) of the 1988 Act,

during the relevant period no prohibition order may be issued as regards any decision, course of action or item of account which led to the report being made.

(2) For the purposes of subsection (1) above the relevant period is the period-

    (a) beginning with the day on which copies of the report are sent, and

    (b) ending with the day (if any) on which the body's consideration of the report under section 115(2) of the 1988 Act begins.

(3) If section 115(3) of the 1988 Act is not complied with, it is immaterial for the purposes of subsection (2)(b) above.]

AMENDMENT

Section 25AA was inserted by the Local Government Finance Act 1988, s.137, Sch.12, para.3(3).

[Effect of and appeals against prohibition orders

25B.–(1) So long as a prohibition order has effect, it shall not be lawful for the body concerned or any officer of that body to make or implement the decision, to take or continue to take the course of action or, as the case may be, to enter the item of account to which the order relates.

(2) A prohibition order-

    (a) takes effect, subject to subsection (5) of section 25A above, on the date specified in the order in accordance with subsection (2)(c) of that section; and

    (b) continues to have effect, subject to any order or decision of the High Court on an appeal under subsection (3) below, until revoked under section 25A(7) above.

(3) Not later than twenty-eight days after the service under section 25A(5) above of a statement of reasons relating to a prohibition order, the body concerned (but not any officer of that body) may appeal against the order to the High Court in accordance with rules of court.

(4) On an appeal against a prohibition order under subsection (3) above, the High Court may make such order as it thinks fit for the payment by the body concerned of expenses incurred by the auditor in connection with the appeal.

(5) Any expenses reasonably incurred by the auditor in or in connection with the issue of a prohibition order shall be recoverable by him from the body concerned.

(6) In this section "the body concerned", in relation to a prohibition order, means the body to which, or to an officer of which, the order is addressed.]

AMENDMENT

Section 25B was inserted by the Local Government Act 1988, s.30(1), Sch.4.

[Supplementary provision as to prohibition orders

25C.–(1) In any case where–

(a) before a prohibition order is issued, a body enters into a contract to dispose of or acquire an interest in land, and

(b) before the disposal or acquisition is completed, a prohibition order takes effect as a result of which it is unlawful for the body to complete the disposal or acquisition,

the existence of the prohibition order shall not prejudice any remedy in damages which may be available to any person by reason of the body's failure to complete the contract.

(2) No action shall lie against an auditor in respect of any loss or damage alleged to have been caused by reason of the issue of a prohibition order which was issued in good faith; but nothing in this subsection affects the right of a court to award costs against an auditor on an appeal under section 25B(3) above.]

AMENDMENT

Section 25C was inserted by the Local Government Act 1988, s.30(1), Sch.4.

[Power of auditor to apply for judicial review

25D.–(1) Subject to section 31(3) of the Supreme Court Act 1981 (no application for judicial review without leave) the auditor appointed in relation to the accounts of a body [other than a health service body] may make an application for judicial review with respect to-

(a) any decision of that body, or

(b) any failure by that body to act,

which (in either case) it is reasonable to believe would have an effect on the accounts of that body.

(2) The existence of the powers conferred on an auditor under this Part of this Act shall not be regarded as a ground for refusing an application falling within subsection (1) above (or an application for leave to make such an application).

(3) On an application for judicial review made as mentioned in subsection (1) above, the court may make such order as it thinks fit for the payment by the body to whose decision the application relates of expenses incurred by the auditor in connection with the application.]

AMENDMENTS

Section 25D was inserted by the Local Government Act 1988, s.30(1) and Sch.4.

The words in square brackets in subs.(1) were inserted by the National Health Service and Community Care Act 1990, s.20, Sch.4, para.17.

Miscellaneous and supplementary

Studies for improving economy etc. in services

26.–(1) The Commission shall undertake or promote comparative and other studies designed to enable it to make recommendations for improving economy, efficiency and effectiveness in the provision of local authority services and of other services provided by bodies whose accounts are required to be audited in accordance with this Part of this Act, and for improving the financial or other management of such bodies.

(2) The Commission may undertake or promote other studies relating to the provision by such bodies of their services besides the studies referred to in subsection (1) above and section 27 below.

(3) The Commission shall publish or otherwise make available its recommendations and the results of any studies under this section [and, in the case of studies relating to a health service body, shall, on request, furnish to the Comptroller and Auditor General, all material relevant to the studies.]

(4) Before undertaking or promoting any study under this section the Commission shall consult such associations of local authorities or other bodies whose accounts are required to be audited in accordance with this Part of this Act as appear to it to be concerned and such associations of employees as appear to it to be appropriate [and, in the case of any health service bodies, the Commission shall also consult the Secretary of State and the Comptroller and Auditor General.]

AMENDMENTS

The words in square brackets in subss.(3) and (4) were inserted by the National Health Service and Community Care Act 1990, s.20, Sch.4, para.18.

Reports on impact of statutory provisions etc.

27.–(1) In addition to the studies referred to in section 26(1) above, the Commission shall undertake or promote studies designed to enable it to prepare reports as to the impact–

(a) of the operation of any particular statutory provision or provisions; or

(b) of any directions or guidance given by a Minister of the Crown (whether pursuant to any such provision or otherwise),

on economy, efficiency and effectiveness in the provision of local authority services and of other services provided by bodies whose accounts are required to be audited in accordance with this Part of this Act [other than health service bodies], or on the financial management of such bodies.

(2) The Commission shall publish or otherwise make available its report of the results of any study under this section, and shall send a copy of any such report to the Comptroller and Auditor General.

(3) Where the Comptroller and Auditor General has received a copy of any such report he may require the Commission to furnish him with any information obtained by it in connection with the preparation of the report, and for that purpose the Commission shall permit any person authorised by him to inspect and make copies of any documents containing any such information; but no information shall be required by the Comptroller and Auditor General under this section in respect of any particular body.

(4) The Comptroller and Auditor General shall from time to time lay before the House of Commons a report of any matters which, in his opinion, arise out of any studies of the Commission under this section and ought to be drawn to the attention of that House.

(5) Before undertaking or promoting any study under this section the Commission shall consult-

(a) the Comptroller and Auditor General;

(b) any Minister of the Crown who appears to it to be concerned; and

(c) such associations of local authorities or other bodies whose accounts are required to be audited in accordance with this Part of this Act as appear to it to be concerned and such associations of employees as appear to it to be appropriate.

[(6) Notwithstanding that the services provided by health service bodies are excluded from the scope of studies under this section, in undertaking or promoting studies under section 26(1) above relating to a health service body, the Commission may take into account the implementation by the body of-

(a) any particular statutory provision or provisions, and

(b) any directions or guidance given by the Secretary of State (whether pursuant to any such provision or otherwise),

but the power conferred by this subsection shall not be construed as entitling the Commission to question the merits of the policy objectives of the Secretary of State.]

AMENDMENTS
Subs.(6) and the words in square brackets in subs.(1) were inserted by the National Health Service and Community Care Act 1990, s.20, Sch.4, para.19.

Furnishing of information and documents to Commission

28.–(1) Without prejudice to any other provision of this Part of this Act, the Commission may require any body whose accounts are required to be audited in accordance with this Part of this Act, and any officer or member of any such body, to furnish the Commission or any person authorised by it with all such information as the Commission or that person may reasonably require for the discharge of the functions under this Part of this Act of the Commission or of that person, including the carrying out of any study under section 26 or 27 above.

(2) For the purpose of assisting the Commission to maintain proper standards in the auditing of the accounts of any such body the Commission may require that body to make available for inspection by or on behalf of the Commission the accounts concerned and such other documents relating to the body as might reasonably be required by an auditor for the purposes of the audit.

(3) Subsections (4) and (5) of section 16 above shall apply in relation to a requirement imposed on any officer or member of a body under subsection (1) above as they apply in relation to a requirement imposed under that section.

Functions of Commission in relation to national health service

28A. [...]

AMENDMENTS
Section 28A was inserted by the Local Government and Housing Act 1989, s.184(1), which was repealed by the National Health Service and Community Care Act 1990, s.66(2) and Sch.10. That repeal was brought into force from 1 October 1990, effectively repealing section 28A from that date.

Miscellaneous functions of Commission

29.–(1) The Commission shall, if so required by the body concerned, make arrangements-

(a) for certifying claims and returns in respect of grants or subsidies made or paid by any Minister of the Crown [or public authority] to any body whose accounts are required to be audited in accordance with this Part of this Act; or

(b) for certifying any account submitted by any such body to any such Minister with a view to obtaining payment under a contract between that body and the Minister; [or

(c) for certifying the body's calculation under paragraph 5(6)(b) of Schedule 8 to the Local Government Finance Act 1988 of the amount of its non-domestic rating contribution for a financial year, and for certifying the amount calculated; or

(d) for certifying any return by the body which, by or under any enactment, is required or authorised to be certified by the body's auditor or under arrangements made by the Commission;

and in paragraph (a) above 'public authority' means a body established by or under the Treaties or by or under any enactment.]

(2) The Commission may, at the request of the body concerned, promote or undertake studies designed to improve economy, efficiency and effectiveness in the management or operations of any body whose accounts are required to be audited in accordance with this Part of this Act, but before making a request under this subsection a body shall consult such associations of employees as appear to the body to be appropriate [or, in the case of a health service body, such other organisations as appear to the body to be appropriate].

(3) The Commission may, with the consent of the Secretary of State and by agreement with the body concerned, undertake the audit of the accounts of any body other than one whose accounts are required to be so audited, being a body which appears to the Secretary of State to be connected with local government [or the National Health Service].

(4) Without prejudice to any applicable statutory provision, any audit carried out pursuant to subsection (3) above shall be carried out in such a manner as the Commission and the body in question may agree; and references in the foregoing provisions of this Part of this Act to an audit carried out thereunder accordingly do not include an audit carried out pursuant to that subsection.

(5) The Commission shall charge the body concerned such fees for services provided under this section as will cover the full cost of providing them.

AMENDMENTS

Subs.(1)(c) was inserted, with effect for financial years beginning in or after 1990, by the Local Government Finance Act 1988, s.137 and Sch.12, para.3(4) and (5).

The words in square brackets in subs.(1)(a), and the whole of subs.(1)(d) and the following words of subs.(1), were inserted by the Local Government and Housing Act 1989, s.184(2).

The words in square brackets in subss.(2) and (3) were inserted by the National Health Service and Community Care Act 1990, s.20, Sch.4, para.20.

Restriction on disclosure of information

30.–(1) No information relating to a particular body or other person and obtained by the Commission or an auditor, or by a person acting on behalf of the Commission or an auditor, pursuant to any provision of this Part of this Act or in the course of any audit or study thereunder shall be disclosed except-

(a) with the consent of the body or person to whom the information relates; or

(b) for the purposes of any functions of the Commission or an auditor under this Part of this Act [or, in the case of a health service body, for the purposes of the functions of the Secretary of State and the Comptroller and Auditor General under the National Health Service Act 1977]; or

(c) for the purposes of any criminal proceedings.

(2) Any person who discloses any information in contravention of subsection (1) above shall be guilty of an offence and liable-

(a) on summary conviction, to imprisonment for a term not exceeding six months or to a fine not exceeding the prescribed sum (as defined in section 32(9) of the Magistrates' Courts Act 1980) or to both; or

(b) on conviction on indictment, to imprisonment for a term not exceeding two years or to a fine or to both.

AMENDMENT

The words in square brackets in subs.(1)(b) were inserted by the National Health Service and Community Care Act 1990, s.20, Sch.4, para.21.

Passenger transport executives and their subsidiaries

31.–(1) The foregoing provisions of this Part of this Act shall apply in relation to a Passenger Transport Executive [...] as they apply in relation to a body to which section 12 above applies, but subject to the following modifications-

(a) the Commission shall under section 13(3) consult the relevant authority instead of the Executive;

(b) the reference in sections 17(2) and (3), 22(1)(a), 23(1)(e) and 24(1) to a local government elector for any such area as is there mentioned shall be construed as a reference to a local government elector for the area of the relevant authority;

(c) the requirements of subsection (3) of section 18 shall apply in relation to the relevant authority as well as the Executive, but subsection (5) of that section shall apply only to the relevant authority;

[(ca) the requirements of section 18A(1) and (2) shall apply to the relevant authority as well as the Executive, but the reference in section 18A(2) to one or more local newspapers circulating in the area of the body or meeting shall be construed as a reference to one or more such newspapers circulating in the area of the relevant authority].

(d) the notice required to be given by section 22(4) shall be given to the relevant authority as well as the Executive.

(2) In subsection (1) above "the relevant authority"-

(a) in relation to a Passenger Transport Executive, means the Passenger Transport Authority for the area for which the Executive is established;[...]

(3) Section 14(1)(a) of the Transport Act 1968[...] (which provide for the keeping of proper accounts and other records) shall have effect subject to any regulations made under section 23, above.

(4) [Where a Passenger Transport Executive have a subsidiary, it shall be their duty to exercise their control over that subsidiary so as to ensure that the subsidiary appoints only auditors who, in addition to being qualified for appointment as such auditors in accordance with section 389 of the Companies Act 1985, are approved by the Commission for appointment as auditors of that subsidiary.]

(5) In this section "subsidiary" means, subject to subsection (6) below, a subsidiary within the meaning of [section 736 of the Companies Act 1985].

(6) Where a company would, if an Executive and any other body or bodies whose accounts are required to be audited in accordance with this Part of this Act were a single body corporate, be a subsidiary of that body corporate, [subsection (4) above shall not apply, but it shall be the joint duty of the Executive and the other body or bodies

concerned to exercise such control over the company as the Executive are required by that subsection to exercise over a subsidiary of theirs.]

AMENDMENTS

The words omitted from subss.(1), (2) and (3) were repealed by the London Regional Transport Act 1984, s.71(3), Sch.7, para.22.

Subs.(4) was substituted by the Transport Act 1985, s.139(2) and Sch.7.

The words in square brackets in subs.(5) were substituted by the Companies Consolidation (Consequential Provisions) Act 1985, Sch.2.

The words in square brackets in subs.(6) were substituted by the Transport Act 1985, s.139(2) and Sch.7, para.22.

Para.(ca) of subs.(1) was inserted by the Local Government Finance (Publicity for Auditors' Reports) Act 1991, s.1(4).

. . . . .

Orders and Regulations

35.–(1) Any power conferred by this Part of this Act to make orders or regulations shall be exercisable by statutory instrument.

(2) Any regulations made under this Part of this Act shall be subject to annulment in pursuance of a resolution of either House of Parliament.

(3) Before making any regulations under section 21(7) or 23 above the Secretary of State shall consult the Commission, such associations of local authorities as appear to him to be concerned and such bodies of accountants as appear to him to be appropriate.

Interpretation of Part III

36.–(1) In this Part of this Act–

"the first appointed day" and "the second appointed day" have the meaning given by section 33, above;

"auditor", in relation to the accounts of any body, means [(except in section 31(4) above)] the person or any of the persons appointed by the Commission to act as auditor in relation to those accounts and, to the extent provided by section 13(8) above, includes a person assisting an auditor under arrangements approved under that provision;

"the Commission" means the Audit Commission for Local Authorities [and the National Health Service] in England and Wales;

"health service body" has the meaning assigned by section 12(5), above;

"recognised fund-holding practice" shall be construed in accordance with section 14 of the National Health Service and Community Care Act 1990];

"statutory provision" means any provision contained in or having effect under any enactment.

(2) Section 270 of the Local Government Act 1972 (general interpretation) shall apply for the interpretation of this Part of this Act.

[(3) In the application of Part III of this Act in relation to the Broads Authority-

(a) any reference to a local government elector shall be construed as a reference to a local government elector for the area of any participating authority (as defined by section 25 of the Norfolk and Suffolk Broads Act 1988); and

(b) the Broads Authority and the Navigation Committee (as so defined) shall each be taken to be a local authority for the purposes of sections 19 and 20.]

AMENDMENTS

In subs.(1) the words in the first square brackets were inserted by the Transport Act 1985, s.139(2), Sch.7, para.22; those in the second and third square brackets by the National Health Service and Community Care Act 1990, s.20, Sch.4, para.23.

Subs.(3) was inserted by the Norfolk and Suffolk Broads Act 1988, s.17.

. . . . .

SCHEDULE 3
THE AUDIT COMMISSION

[Schedule 3 remains as set out in the main text except for the paragraphs printed below as amended.]

3.–(3) No direction shall be given by the Secretary of State and no information shall be required by him under this paragraph in respect of any particular body whose accounts are required to be audited in accordance with Part III of this Act; and before giving any direction under this paragraph the Secretary of State shall consult the Commission, such associations of local authorities as appear to him to be concerned [or, as the case may require, such organisations connected with the health service as appear to him to be appropriate and (in either case)] such bodies of accountants as appear to him to be appropriate.

AMENDMENT

The words in square brackets were inserted by the National Health Service and Community Care Act 1990, s.20, Sch.4, para.24.

. . . . .

9.[–(1) Subject to sub-paragraph (2), below] it shall be the duty of the Commission so to manage its affairs that its income from fees and otherwise will, taking one year with another, be not less than its expenditure properly chargeable to its income and expenditure account.

[(2) Sub-paragraph (1) above shall apply separately with respect to the functions of the Commission in relation to health service bodies and its functions in relation to other bodies.]

AMENDMENTS

Sub-para.(2) and the words in square brackets in sub-para.(1) were inserted by the National Health Service and Community Care Act 1990, s.20, Sch.4, para.24(2).

A.2. NATIONAL HEALTH SERVICE ACT 1977

Accounts and Audit

98.–(1) Accounts, in such form as the Secretary of State may with the approval of the Treasury direct, shall be kept by-

(a) every Regional Health Authority;

(b) [...]

[(bb)   every District Health Authority];

[(bbb) every NHS trust];

(c) every special health authority;

[(cc)   every [Family Health Services Authority]];

(d) all special trustees appointed in pursuance of section 29(1) of the National Health Service Reorganisation Act 1973 and section 95(1), above;

[(dd) any trustees for an NHS Trust appointed in pursuance of section 11 of the National Health Service and Community Care Act 1990; and]

(e) the [Dental Practice Board].

Those accounts shall be audited by auditors [appointed by the Audit Commission for Local Authorities and the National Health Service in England and Wales and the Comptroller] and Auditor General may examine all such accounts and any records relating to them, and any report of the auditor on them.

(2) Every such body shall prepare and transmit to the Secretary of State in respect of each financial year annual accounts in such form as the Secretary of State may with the approval of the Treasury direct. [...]

[(2A) The accounts prepared and transmitted by a District Health Authority in pursuance of subsection (2) above shall include annual accounts of a Community Health Council if-

(a) the Council is established for the Authority's district; or

(b) the Authority is the prescribed Authority in relation to the Council.]

[(2B) So far as relates to allotted sums paid to the members of a fund-holding practice-

(a) accounts shall be kept in such form as the Secretary of State may with the approval of the Treasury direct;

(b) the Comptroller and Auditor General may examine the accounts and the records relating to them and any report of the auditor on them;

(c) in respect of each financial year, annual accounts in such form as the Secretary of State may with the approval of the Treasury direct shall be prepared and submitted to the relevant Family Health Services Authority; and

(d) in respect of each financial year, each Family Health Services Authority shall prepare, in such form as the Secretary of State may with the approval of the Treasury direct, and include in its own accounts, a summarised version of the accounts submitted to the Authority under paragraph (c) above].

[(2B) In preparing its annual accounts in pursuance of subsection (2) above, an NHS trust shall comply with any directions given by the Secretary of State with the approval of the Treasury as to–

(a) the methods and principles according to which the accounts are to be prepared; and

(b) the information to be given in the accounts.]

(3) [...]

(4) The Secretary of State shall prepare in respect of each financial year-

(a) in such form as the Treasury may direct, summarised accounts of [the bodies mentioned in subsection (1) above, other than the [Dental Practice Board]];

(b) in such form and containing such information as the Treasury may direct, a statement of the accounts of the [Dental Practice Board];

and shall transmit them on or before 30th November in each year to the Comptroller and Auditor General, who shall examine and certify them, and lay copies of them together with his report on them before both Houses of Parliament.

[(5) In subsection (2B) above "recognised fund-holding practice" and "allotted sum" have the same meaning as in section 15 of the National Health Service and Community Care Act 1990.]

AMENDMENTS

Subs.(1)(bb) was added by the Health Services Act 1980, Sch.1.

Subs.(1)(cc) was added, and the words in the outer square brackets in subs.(4) substituted, by the Health and Social Services and Social Security Adjudications Act 1983, Sch.5, para.3.

Subs.(2A) was added by the Health and Social Security Act 1984, s.3. Words in subs.(2) were repealed by *ibid*, Sch.7.

The words "Dental Practice Board" in subss.(1)(e) and 4(a), (b) were substituted by the Health and Medicines Act 1988, s.12(1).

The first subs.(2B) and subs.(5) were inserted, subs.(3) repealed, and the words in square brackets in the last sentence of subs.(1) substituted, by the National Health Service and Community Care Act 1990, s.20(2). Subs.1(b) was repealed by *ibid*, Sch.10. The words in the inner square brackets in subs.(1)(cc) were substituted by *ibid*, s.2(1). Subs.(1)(bbb) and the second subs.(2B) were inserted by *ibid*, Sch.2, para.24. Subs.1(dd) was inserted by *ibid*, s.11(7). It is understood that the error in enacting two subsections with the number (2B) can be corrected only by further legislation.

A.3. LOCAL GOVERNMENT AND HOUSING ACT 1989

Confidentiality of staff records

11.–(1) Nothing in section 17 of the Local Government Finance Act 1982 or section 79 of the Local Government Act 1985 (public inspection of accounts etc.) or in section 101 or 106 of the Local Government (Scotland) Act 1973 (which makes corresponding provision for Scotland) shall entitle any person-

   (a) to inspect so much of any document as contains personal information about a member of the relevant body's staff; or

   (b) to require any such information to be disclosed in answer to any question.

(2) Information shall be regarded as personal information about a member of the relevant body's staff if it relates specifically to a particular individual and is available to that body for reasons connected with the fact-

   (a) that that individual holds or has held any office or employment under that body; or

   (b) that payments or other benefits in respect of any office or employment under any other person are or have been made or provided to that individual by that body.

(3) In this section-

   "document" includes accounts, books, deeds, contracts, bills, vouchers and re- ceipts; and

   "relevant body" in relation to accounts which are required to be audited in accord- ance with Part III of the said Act of 1982 or Part VII of the said Act of 1973, means the body whose accounts are required to be audited or, as the case may be, the Common Council of the City of London;

and references inthis section to a payment made or benefit provided to an individual in respect of any office or employment include references to a payment made or benefit provided to him in respect of his ceasing to hold the office or employment.

(4) This section shall have effect only in relation to-

   (a) the inspection of, or of documents relating to, accounts for periods beginning on or after 1st April 1990; and

   (b) the disclosure of information in answer to questions about such accounts.

A.4. NATIONAL HEALTH SERVICE AND COMMUNITY CARE ACT 1990

Extension of functions etc. of Audit Commission to cover the health service

20.–(1) Part III of the Local Government Finance Act 1982 (the Audit Commission for Local Authorities in England and Wales - in this section referred to as "the Commission") shall have effect subject to the amendments in Schedule 4 to this Act, being amendments–

(a) to extend the functions of the Commission to cover health authorities and other bodies established under this Act or the principal Act;

(b) to alter the title and constitution of the Commission to reflect its wider role; and

(c) to make provision consequential on or supplemental to the amendments referred to in paragraphs (a) and (b) above.

[The amendments made by Sch.4 to Part III of the 1982 Act have been incorporated therein, above.

Subs.(2) made amendments to s.98, National Health Service Act 1977 which have been incorporated therein, above.]

(3) If the person who is for the time being the auditor, within the meaning of Part III of the Local Government Finance Act 1982, in relation to the accounts of a health service body, within the meaning of that Part, has reason to believe that the body, or any officer of the body,-

(a) is about to make, or has made, a decision which involves or would involve the incurring of expenditure which is unlawful, or

(b) is about to take, or has taken, a course of action which, if pursued to its conclusion, would be unlawful and likely to cause a loss or deficiency,

he shall refer the matter forthwith to the Secretary of State.

(4) It shall be the duty of the Commission to make, by such date as the Secretary of State may determine, an offer of employment by the Commission to each person employed in the civil service of the State in connection with the audit of the accounts of any of the bodies specified in section 98(1) of the principal Act whose name is notified to the Commission by the Secretary of State for the purposes of this subsection; and the terms of the offer must be such that they are, taken as a whole, not less favourable to the person to whom the offer is made than the terms on which he is employed on the date on which the offer is made.

(5) An offer made in pursuance of subsection (4) above shall not be revocable during the period of three months beginning with the date on which it is made.

(6) Where a person becomes an officer or servant of the Commission in consequence of subsection (4) above, then, for the purposes of the Employment Protection (Consolidation) Act 1978, his period of employment in the civil service of the State shall count as a period of employment by the Commission and the change of employment shall not break the continuity of the period of employment.

(7) Where a person ceases to be employed as mentioned in subsection (4) above-

(a) on becoming an officer or servant of the Commission in consequence of an offer made in pursuance of that subsection, or

(b) having unreasonably refused such an offer,

he shall not, on ceasing to be so employed, be treated for the purposes of any scheme under section 1 of the Superannuation Act 1972 as having been retired on redundancy.

(8) Without prejudice to any express amendment made by this Act, on and after the day appointed for the coming into force of this subsection, any reference in any

enactment (including an enactment comprised in subordinate legislation) to the Audit Commission for Local Authorities in England and Wales shall be construed as a reference to the Audit Commission for Local Authorities and the National Health Service in England and Wales.

APPENDIX B

STATUTORY INSTRUMENTS

B.1. THE ACCOUNTS AND AUDIT REGULATIONS 1983
(S.I. 1983/1761)

[These regulations remain as set out in the main text except for the paragraphs printed below as amended].

2.–(2) Any reference in these regulations to accounts shall, in relation to the Common Council of the City of London, be construed as a reference to the accounts [referred to in section 12(3) of the 1982 Act].

AMENDMENT

The words in square brackets were substituted by the Accounts and Audit (Amendment) Regulations 1990, S.I. 1990/435, applying to accounts from 1990/1.

7.–[(2) This paragraph applies to the following bodies:-

(a) the council of a county, a district or a London borough and the Council of the Isles of Scilly;

(aa) a joint authority [...] and an authority established by the Waste Regulation and Disposal (Authorities) Order 1985;

(b) any committee of a body mentioned in sub-paragraphs (a) or (aa) above which is required to keep separate accounts;

(c) any joint committee of two or more bodies mentioned in sub-paragraphs (a) or (aa) above;

(cc) [the Broads Authority];

(d) any combined police authority; and

(e) any fire authority constituted by a combination scheme.]

AMENDMENTS

Paragraph (2) was substituted by the Accounts and Audit (Amendment) Regulations 1986, S.I. 1986/1271.

The words omitted from sub-paragraph (2)(aa) were deleted in relation to accounts from 1990/1 by S.I. 1990/435.

Sub-paragraph (2)(cc) was inserted in relation to accounts from 1989/90 by S.I. 1990/435.

11.–(3) In the case of a parish council, parish meeting, community council, joint committee of the councils of two or more parishes or communities or of the Council of the Isles of Scilly, the body or as the case may be the chairman of the meeting may, instead of giving notice under paragraph (1), display a notice containing the requisite information in a conspicuous place or places in the area to which the accounts relate for a period of at least 14 days immediately prior to [the period during which the accounts and other documents are made available under regulation 9].

AMENDMENT
The words in square brackets were substituted by S.I. 1986/1271.

14.–[(6) A parish council, a community council, a joint committee of the councils of two or more parish or community councils, the Council of the Isles of Scilly or the chairman of a parish meeting may, instead of giving notice under paragraph (1), display a notice containing the requisite information in a conspicuous place or places in the areas to which the accounts relate for a period of not less than 28 days commencing at the earliest possible date after the conclusion of the audit or, as the case may be, the meeting at which the auditor's report was taken into consideration.

(6A) A parish or community council with a population of less than 2,000, a joint committee of the councils of two or more such parish or community councils, the Council of the Isles of Scilly or the chairman of the parish meeting may, instead of giving notice under paragraph (2), display a notice containing the requisite information in a conspicuous place or places in the areas to which the accounts relate for a period of not less than 28 days commencing at the earliest possible date after the meeting at which the auditor's report was taken into consideration].

(7) Where a notice is displayed under [paragraphs (6) and (6A)] in relation to an auditor's report, as soon as possible after the commencement of the period mentioned in that paragraph the body, or chairman as the case may be, shall notify the auditor in writing that a notice has been so displayed.

AMENDMENTS
Paragraph (6) and the words in square brackets in paragraph (7) were substituted, and paragraph (6A) was added, by S.I. 1986/1271.

16.– Where, under section 22 of the 1982 Act, the Commission directs an auditor to hold an extraordinary audit of accounts of a body, the body, or in the case of a parish meeting the chairman of the meeting, shall give notice by advertisement of the right of any local government elector for the area to which the accounts relate or any representative of his to attend before the auditor and make objections to any of those accounts; and [regulation 11(4)] shall apply in relation to any notice under this paragraph as it applies in relation to a notice under regulation 11(1).

AMENDMENT
The words in square brackets were substituted by S.I. 1986/1271.

B.2.   **RULES OF THE SUPREME COURT 1965**

ORDER 98

LOCAL GOVERNMENT FINANCE ACT 1982, PART III

Interpretation

1. In this Order "the Act" means the Local Government Finance Act 1982 and a section referred to by number means the section so numbered in that Act.

Application by auditor for declaration

2.–(1) Any application for a declaration under section 19(1) of the Act that an item of account is contrary to law shall be made by originating motion.

(2) Notice of the motion shall be served on the body to whose accounts the application relates and on any person against whom an order is sought under section 19(2).

(3) Not later than seven days after lodging the notice of motion in the Crown Office in accordance with Order 57, rule 2, the applicant shall file in that office an affidavit stating the facts on which he intends to rely at the hearing of the application.

(4) A motion under this rule shall be entered for hearing within six weeks after the notice has been lodged in the Crown Office but, unless the Court otherwise directs, the application shall not be heard sooner than 28 days after service of the notice.

Appeal against decision of auditor

3.–(1) Notice of motion by which an appeal is brought under section 19(4) or section 20(3) against the decision of an auditor shall be served on–

(a) the auditor who for the time being has responsibility for the audit of the accounts of the body in relation to whom the appeal relates;

(b) that body; and

(c) in the case of an appeal against a decision not to certify under section 20(1) that a sum or amount is due from another person, that person.

(2) Order 55, rules 4(2) and 5, shall apply to the appeal with the modification that the period of 28 days mentioned in the said rule 4(2) shall be calculated from the day on which the appellant received the auditor's statement of the reasons for his decision pursuant to a requirement under section 19(4) or section 20(2).

(3) Not later than seven days after lodging notice of motion in the Crown Office in accordance with Order 57, rule 2, the appellant must file in that office an affidavit stating–

(a) the reasons stated by the auditor for his decision;

(b) the date on which he received the auditor's statement;

(c) the facts on which he intends to rely at the hearing of the appeal;

(d) in the case of a decision not to apply for a declaration, such facts within the appellant's knowledge as will enable the Court to consider whether to exercise the powers conferred on it by section 19(2).

General provisions

4.–(1) Any proceedings in which the jurisdiction conferred on the High Court by section 19 or section 20 of the Act is invoked shall be assigned to the Queen's Bench Division and be heard by a single judge, unless the Court directs that the matter shall be heard by a Divisional Court; and the Court may, at any stage and without prejudice to its powers under Order 15, direct that any officer or member of the body to whose accounts the application or appeal relates be joined as a respondent.

(2) Except in so far as the Court directs that the evidence on any such application or appeal shall be given orally, it shall be given by affidavit.

(3) The applicant or appellant must forthwith after filing any affidavit under rule 2(3) or 3(3) serve a copy thereof on every respondent and any person intending to oppose the application or appeal must, not less than four days before the hearing, serve on the applicant or appellant a copy of any affidavit filed by him in opposition to the motion.

(4) Except by leave of the Court, no affidavit may be used at the hearing unless a copy thereof was served in accordance with paragraph (3).

AMENDMENTS

Order 98 was substituted by Rules of the Supreme Court (Amendment No.2) 1974 (S.I. 1974/1115). Rules 2(1) and 4(1) were further substituted by Rules of the Supreme Court (Amendment No.4) 1980 (S.I. 1980/2000) with effect from 12 January 1981, and further amendments were effected by Rules of the Supreme Court (Amendment No.2) 1985 (S.I. 1985/846) in the light of the coming into force of the Local Government Finance Act 1982 for accounts from 1983/4 onwards.

B.3.   # COUNTY COURT RULES 1981

ORDER 49, rule 10

LOCAL GOVERNMENT FINANCE ACT 1982

10.–(1) In this rule a section referred to by number means the section so numbered in the Local Government Finance Act 1982.

(2) Proceedings in a county court under section 19 or section 20 shall be commenced in the court for the district in which the principal office of the body to whose accounts the application relates (in this rule referred to as "the body concerned") is situated.

(3) An originating application for a declaration under section 19(1) shall state the facts on which the applicant intends to rely at the hearing of the application and the respondents to the application shall be the body concerned and any person against whom an order is sought under section 19(2).

(4) An appeal under section 19(4) or section 20(3) against a decision of an auditor shall be brought within 28 days of the receipt by the appellant of the auditor's statement of the reasons for his decision.

(5) The request for entry of an appeal to which paragraph (4) relates shall state-

    (a) the reasons stated by the auditor for his decision;

    (b) the date on which the appellant received the auditor's statement;

    (c) the facts on which the appellant intends to rely at the hearing of the appeal; and

    (d) in the case of a decision not to apply for a declaration, such facts within the appellant's knowledge as will enable the court to consider whether to exercise the powers conferred on it by section 19(2).

(6) The respondents to the appeal shall be–

    (i) the auditor who for the time being has responsibility for the audit of the accounts of the body concerned;

    (ii) the body concerned; and

    (iii)in the case of an appeal against a decision not to certify under section 20(1) that a sum or amount is due from any person, that person.

(7) Without prejudice to its powers under Order 15, the court may at any stage of an application or appeal under section 19 or section 20 direct that any officer or member of the body concerned be joined as a respondent.

AMENDMENTS

This rule was enacted by the County Court Rules 1981 (S.I. 1981/ 1687), repeating the provision of the former C.C.R. O.46, r.26. It was amended by the County Court (Amendment) Rules 1985 (S.I. 1985/ 566) in the light of the coming into force of the Local Government Finance Act 1982 for accounts from 1983/4 onwards.

As to the effect of the High Court and County Courts Jurisdiction Order 1991, S.I. 1991/724, see 9.2-4, 9.6, above.

APPENDIX C

CODE OF AUDIT PRACTICE FOR LOCAL AUTHORITIES AND THE NATIONAL HEALTH SERVICE IN ENGLAND AND WALES

INTRODUCTION

1. Section 14 of the Local Government Finance Act 1982 (the Act) as amended by the National Health Service and Community Care Act 1990 requires the Audit Commission for Local Authorities and the National Health Service in England and Wales (the Commission) to prepare and keep under review a code of audit practice prescribing the way in which auditors are to carry out their functions under Part III of the Act. The code must be approved by a resolution of each House of Parliament at intervals of not more than five years and this code revises and replaces the code which came into effect on 7 July 1988.

2. The code must embody what appears to the Commission to be the best professional practice with respect to the standards, procedures and techniques to be adopted by auditors, and cannot come into force until approved by a resolution of each House of Parliament. For the audit of local authorities, the code must be read in conjunction with any regulations for the time being in force under section 23 of the Act. In the case of health service bodies, the code must be read in conjunction with any directions under section 98(2) of the National Health Service Act 1977 and the National Health Service and Community Care Act 1990.

3. In drawing up a suitably prescriptive code, the Commission necessarily omits explanatory material. This code draws upon *The Auditing Standards and Guidelines*, and the Auditing Guidelines *Applicability to the Public Sector of Auditing Standards and Guidelines, and The Impact of Regulations on Public Sector Audits* developed by the Auditing Practices Committee of the Consultative Committee of the Accountancy Bodies.

4. In addition to the auditor's continuing responsibility to assess the legality and regularity of financial affairs, the Commission emphasises the auditor's value for money responsibilities and requires auditors to demonstrate a value for money content in their audits. The concern that the authority has made proper arrangements to secure economy, efficiency and effectiveness should influence the auditor throughout the audit.

5. The Act provides for the auditor to be appointed by the Commission - not by the authorities; and reappointment will depend on the Commission's judgement of how well the auditor has discharged the duties imposed under the Act, and met the requirements of this code. However, as the code makes clear, the auditor will be expected to discharge all professional responsibilities independently, both of the Commission and its officers and of the authority.

6. There will be occasions in which aspects of the code are inappropriate to the audit of certain bodies; in local government in respect of the audit of authorities such as parish councils, parish meetings, community councils, and internal drainage boards, and in the

health service, bodies such as practice fund holders whose accounts will be summarised in the accounts of family health service authorities, and special trustees. All these authorities are referred to in the code as 'non-principal' authorities.

7. The main provisions of the code are in five parts. The first sets out the duties of an auditor appointed by the Commission; the second relates to the conduct of the audit; the third sets out the auditor's reporting responsibilities; the fourth describes the particular responsibilities with regard to the audit of local authorities and other local government bodies subject to audit under Part III of the Act (referred to in this code as 'local authorities'; the fifth describes the auditor's specific responsibilities with regard to the audit of health service bodies subject to audit under Part III of the Act (referred to in this code as 'health authorities').

1. DUTIES OF AN AUDITOR

8. The standards, procedures and techniques included in this code have been prescribed by the Commission in pursuance of the Commission's basic approach and in the light of the particular statutory duties imposed on an auditor by Part III of the Act. This basic approach requires the auditor:

(a)   To recognise that the requirements for the audit of public funds are different from those applicable to the audit of commercial undertakings. The auditor must satisfy himself as to the legality of items of account, that proper practices have been observed, and that in compiling the accounts different sections of the public whose interests may be affected by them have been fairly treated.

(b)   To be concerned both with the form and regularity of accounts, and with the arrangements for securing economy, efficiency and effectiveness in the use of public funds.

(c)   To take a broad-based, analytical approach to the work. The starting point must be an overview of the characteristics of the authority, the responsibilities and problems it faces, and the health of its administration and organisation. Only then will it be possible to identify areas meriting particular attention and to plan the audit work effectively. The same principle should be applied when any particular audit task is undertaken. A commonsense general appreciation of the subject matter is essential before any detailed checks are undertaken.

(d)   To be concerned for action. The auditor's work must be characterised by a constructive attitude; his aim must be to assist members of authorities and their officers, but the auditor must not hesitate to pursue conclusions even to the point of qualification or report in the public interest where necessary.

(e)   To co-operate with other auditors, internal as well as external, and the Commission in order to ensure that knowledge of good practice is transferred effectively from one authority to another, and that a consistent audit approach is adopted.

9. At all times the auditor must remember that his responsibility under this code will be adequately discharged only by a fundamental commitment to the Commission's basic approach as set out in paragraph 8 above, and by the auditor's independence, due professional care and a recognition of the public interest.

Independence

10. The following standard applies as regards independence: "In order that the auditor's opinions, conclusions, judgements and recommendations will be and will be seen to be impartial, the auditor and the audit staff must be independent of the authority and

maintain an independent and objective attitude of mind." The auditor must ensure that independence is not impaired in any way. The following should be avoided:

(a)   Official, professional or personal relationships the nature and effect of which might cause the auditor to limit the extent or character of the audit.

(b)   Involvement in a decision making or management capacity in the operation of the authority being audited.

(c)   Any substantial financial interest, direct or indirect, in the transactions of or services provided by the authority (other than on an arm's-length basis - e.g. as community chargepayer or taxpayer).

The auditor must also guard against any improper attempt to influence his judgement as to the content of any report in the public interest or the opinion on the statement of accounts.

11. Where an appointed auditor of an authority, or any firm with which the auditor is associated, carries out additional work for that authority, allegations may be made to the effect that the acceptance of such additional work may impair the auditor's independence. To protect auditors from such allegations, except for the two exceptions mentioned below, an appointed auditor (or a firm or any organisation in which the auditor has an interest) may not undertake any work, in addition to that relating directly to the discharge of an auditor's duties for that authority. The two exceptions are:

(a)   Where the cost of the additional work does not exceed a de minimis value of £10,000 in total in each financial year; this amount will be revised annually by the Commission.

(b)   Where the authority and the appointed auditor are able to satisfy the Commission both that such additional work will not run the risk of impairing the auditor's independence and also that it should be performed by the firm in which the auditor has an interest, rather than by any other firm, to ensure economy and efficiency in the utilisation of the authority's resources.

Professional Care

12. The following standard applies as regards due professional care: "The auditor shall exercise due professional care in carrying out and reporting upon the audit." The auditor is expected to bring reasonable care and skill to each audit according to its circumstances and to carry out such enquiries, checks and tests as would seem to be necessary. Examples of what is reasonable care and skill include the auditor:

(a)   Taking reasonable steps to obtain any information which would be relevant to the audit.

(b)   Having regard to the lessons of past audit experience, and that of other auditors, in devising the audit approach.

(c)   Taking into consideration any unusual circumstances or relationships and giving special attention to any material features of the audit which may be affected by unusual characteristics..

(d)   Looking out for and recognising unfamiliar situations.

(e)   Taking steps to resolve any doubtful impressions or unanswered questions concerning features of the audit material to the opinion.

(f)   Keeping up to date with developments in professional matters.

(g)   Ensuring that the audit is staffed with sufficient suitably qualified and experienced personnel and that the work of the staff is properly reviewed.

(h)   Preserving where appropriate the confidentiality of sensitive information received during the audit.

Audit Objectives

13. In providing a service to authorities and the public in accordance with the Act and this code, the auditor will give an independent assessment of:

(a)   Whether the statement of accounts presents fairly the financial position of the authority.

(b)   The general financial standing of the authority.

(c)   The adequacy of the financial systems.

(d)   The adequacy of the arrangements in place for preventing and detecting fraud and corruption.

(e)   The performance of particular services.

(f)   The effectiveness of management arrangements.

14. The auditor will discharge these responsibilities by providing:

(a)   A certificate that the audit has been completed in accordance with statutory requirements.

(b)   An annual opinion on the statement of accounts.

(c)   A management letter addressed to members which will give a summary of the audit activities and details of the significant matters which have arisen. It should also provide an agenda for a meeting with members.

(d)   Where appropriate a report dealing with matters considered by the auditor to be of public interest.

(e)   Reports to the officers and where appropriate members on the results of any nationally based value for money studies performed, any local value for money studies undertaken, any assessment of a particular aspect of overall management arrangements carried out and if relevant the impact of new legislation.

(f)   Reports or memoranda to the officers following the conclusion of the assessment of the controls over and the operation of the financial systems and the examination of the statement of accounts.

In this way the auditor will provide the authority with the appropriate degree of assurance on whether it has properly discharged its stewardship of public monies.

2. CONDUCTING THE AUDIT

15. The auditor must plan the audit in detail, deciding where to concentrate enquiries and on the allocation of resources in order to achieve a balance of work between regularity and value for money aspects of the audit. The audit must be carried out in a professional and timely fashion and the result must be reported to the authority concerned in such a way as to inform members of the authority and their officers of the nature and grounds for any concerns and to encourage any corrective action that may be required.

16. At every audit, the auditor must comply with the Auditors' Operational Standard developed by the Auditing Practices Committee, which states:

"Planning, controlling and recording

The auditor should adequately plan, control and record his work.

Accounting systems

The auditor should ascertain the enterprise's system of recording and processing transactions and assess its adequacy as a basis for the preparation of financial statements.

Audit evidence

The auditor should obtain relevant and reliable audit evidence sufficient to enable him to draw reasonable conclusions therefrom.

Internal controls

If the auditor wishes to place reliance on any internal controls, he should ascertain and evaluate those controls and perform compliance tests on their operation.

Review of financial statements

The auditor should carry out such a review of the financial statements as is sufficient, in conjunction with the conclusions drawn from the other audit evidence obtained, to give him a reasonable basis for his opinion on the financial statements."

Planning

17. In planning the audit to achieve the objectives set out in paragraph 13, matters which the auditor should take into account include:

(a)   Information from within the authority such as budgets, minutes of meetings, internal audit plans and discussions with officers and members.

(b)   Information circulated by the Commission.

(c)   The effects of any changes in legislation or accounting practice affecting the financial statements.

(d)   The results of previous audit work and experience and an awareness of relevant national issues, local policies and matters of public interest.

18. The conclusions arising from the planning process should be documented and a detailed time and staff budget prepared. The auditor should discuss the main features of the audit with the appropriate officers of the authority.

Controlling and recording

19. The auditor needs to be satisfied that at each audit the work is being performed to an acceptable standard. The most important elements of control of an audit are the direction and supervision of the audit staff and the review of the work they have done. The degree of supervision required depends on the complexity of the assignment and the experience and proficiency of the audit staff. The work of specialist staff should be co-ordinated with the work of others engaged on the audit.

20. The control procedures established should be designed and applied to ensure the following:

(a)   Audit staff of all levels clearly understand their responsibilities and the objective of the procedures which they are expected to perform. Audit staff should be informed of any matters identified during the planning stage that may affect the nature, extent or timing of the procedures they are to perform. They should be instructed to bring to the attention of those to whom they are responsible any significant accounting or auditing problems that they encounter.

(b)   Audit records should always be sufficiently complete and detailed to enable an experienced auditor with no previous connection with the audit to ascertain from them what work was performed and to support the conclusions reached.

Accounting Systems and Internal Controls

21. The auditor should assess the internal controls in those systems which are necessary to form an opinion on the accounts. The auditor will also review the internal controls that are designed to prevent and detect fraud and irregularities. The auditor should report on any significant control weaknesses identified in the major financial systems.

22. In deciding on the approach to audit work on accounting systems and internal controls, the auditor will be guided by the significance of the system and the controls in relation to the statement of accounts of the authority taken as a whole. The auditor will need to concentrate on significant systems and controls for the purpose of supporting the audit opinion whereas the auditor's wider role suggests that a rotational approach be adopted for those of less significance. At all stages of the work, the auditor should make maximum use of analytical review and computer assisted audit techniques where appropriate.

Audit Evidence

23. The auditor should obtain relevant and reliable audit evidence from which to draw reasonable conclusions to fulfil the requirements of this code. Sources of audit evidence include the accounting systems and underlying documentation of the authority, officers and members, suppliers and others who have dealings with the authority including the general public. In obtaining audit evidence the auditor must take account of the materiality of the matter under consideration.

Financial Statements

24. The auditor should review the financial statements so that when combined with the results of reviewing the financial systems and carrying out substantive testing of the figures in the statements there will be a reasonable basis for giving an opinion whether the statements present fairly the financial position of the authority and its income and expenditure for the year. In particular the auditor should be satisfied on the following matters in relation to the statements:

(a)   For local authorities, the provisions of the *Code of Practice on Local Authority Accounting* issued by the Chartered Institute of Public Finance and Accountancy and available from the address given in the footnote below* have been complied with, except in situations in which for justifiable reasons it is impracticable or, exceptionally, would be inappropriate or give a misleading view.

(b)   For local authorities, any accounting policies that have a material effect, but which are not covered by the *Code of Practice on Local Authority Accounting* referred to in (a), are appropriate to the circumstances of the authority and comply with good practice.

(c)   For health authorities, the Accounting Standards issued and approved by the Secretary of State have been complied with, except in situations in which for justifiable reasons it is impracticable or, exceptionally, would be inappropriate or give a misleading view.

(d) For health authorities, any accounting policies that have a material effect which are not covered by the Accounting Standards issued and approved by the Secretary of State and referred to in (c), are appropriate to the circumstances of the authority and comply with good practice.

(e) The figures are not overstated or understated by a material amount.

(f) The description of the figures is neither misleading nor ambiguous.

(g) There is compliance with statutory and other requirements applicable to the accounts of the authority.

(h) There is adequate disclosure of all appropriate material items.

(i) The information contained in the statement of accounts is suitably classified and presented.

* Copies of the Code of Practice on Local Accounting may be obtained from CIPFA at 3 Robert Street, London WC2N 6BH.

25. If the auditor is not satisfied on any of the matters referred to in the above paragraph which are material to the statement of accounts, the opinion should be qualified. The format of the opinion is explained in part 3 of this code "Reporting the Audit".

26. In addition to the above the auditor has particular responsibilities in relation to fraud and irregularities, corruption, legality and value for money, which are discussed below.

Fraud and Irregularities

27. The term 'fraud and irregularities' is here used to refer to intentional distortions of financial statements and accounting records and to misappropriation of assets, whether or not accompanied by distortion of financial statements and accounting records.

28. The primary responsibility for the prevention and detection of fraud and irregularities rests with management who should institute an adequate system of internal control, including segregation of duties, proper authorisation procedures, and an effective internal audit function. The auditor's responsibility is to review, in accordance with the requirements of this code, the arrangements made by management.

29. The resources available to the auditor have to be put to best effect and the prevention and detection of fraud and irregularities is only one of many claims on audit time. However, the integrity of public funds is at all times a matter of general concern and the auditor should be aware that this function is seen to be an important safeguard. In this area, the auditor has the following special responsibilities:

(a) The audit should be planned so that there is a reasonable expectation of detecting material misstatements in the statement of accounts resulting from fraud and irregularities. Thus, the auditor should endeavour to identify and pay special attention to those activities of the authority which are particularly exposed to the risk of fraud and irregularities which, if present, could result in a material effect on the finances of the authority or a material misstatement in the statement of accounts.

(b) In the review of internal control, in the testing of transactions, and in the review of published and other statistics, the auditor should be alert constantly to the possibility of fraud and irregularities. Management's attention should be drawn to any weakness in internal control which facilitates fraud and irregularities and to those activities which call for occasional deterrent spot checks by management.

(c)   Any indication of fraud and irregularities from whatever source and whatever the likely amount involved should be followed up forthwith. In most cases the auditor's responsibility will be discharged by informing the authority and ensuring that they take the necessary action.

(d)   Any relevant information circulated by the Commission should be studied, any necessary conclusions drawn and action taken as appropriate.

(e)   Attention should be drawn to any steps necessary for management to discharge its responsibility for the prevention of fraud and irregularities, in particular in those areas which are specially sensitive in terms of the public interest.

Corruption

30. The term 'corrupt practices' is defined for the purpose of this code as the offering, giving, soliciting or acceptance of an inducement or reward which may influence the actions taken by the authority, its members or officers. It is the duty of the authority to take reasonable steps to limit the possibility of corrupt practices; and it is the responsibility of the auditor to review the adequacy of the measures taken by the authority, to test compliance and to draw attention to any weaknesses or omissions.

31. Areas where corrupt practices may be found and to which the auditor should pay special attention include tendering and award of contracts, settlement of contractors' final accounts and claims, pecuniary interests of members and officers, secondary employment of staff which may influence their work for the authority, canvassing for appointments, hospitality, pressure selling, the award of permissions, planning consents and licences, and the disposal of assets.

32. The auditor should establish whether the authority has taken reasonable steps to limit the possibility of corrupt practices, and in particular that it:

(a)   Adopts and keeps under review standing orders and financial regulations, particularly those relating to contracts for work and the supply of goods and services, and regularly investigates significant purchases where the lowest tender was not accepted.

(b)   Keeps under review any circumstances in which particular contractors seem to be preferred, particularly where it is not possible or reasonable to have competitive tendering.

(c)   Issues appropriate instructions to regulate the handling of contracts, including such matters as the certification of the receipt of goods or services and the certification of the amounts due.

(d)   Issues appropriate standing orders, financial regulations or codes of conduct to advise members and officers of their personal responsibilities under statute and any local relevant rules.

(e)   Has clear and well publicised arrangements for receiving and investigating complaints of corruption.

(f)   Ensures that internal audit tests compliance with and the effectiveness of the procedures laid down, and in particular examines contract procedures.

33. Once the auditor has reviewed the measures taken by the authority and is satisfied as to their reasonableness the annual task is to hold a watching brief. The auditor should take note of any evidence from whatever source which may indicate the possibility of corrupt practices. Where necessary in the public interest, any such evidence should be referred for further investigation by the appropriate body which according to the circumstances might be the authority or the police.

Legality

34. The auditor should keep under review the legality of the authority's transactions, and be aware of the requirements of existing and new statutory provisions. The specific requirements when auditing local authorities are explained in part 4 and for health authorities in part 5 of this code.

Value for Money

35. In addition to the auditor's responsibility towards the regularity of an authority's accounts the Act imposes a responsibility in the field of the value for money of an authority's transactions. Section 15(1) of the Act requires that 'an auditor shall by examination of the accounts and otherwise satisfy himself.... that the body whose accounts are being audited has made proper arrangements for securing economy, efficiency and effectiveness in its use of resources'. This responsibility is discharged by incorporating a value for money element to the audit.

(*Economy* may be defined as the terms under which the authority acquires human and material resources. An economical operation acquires these resources in the appropriate quality and quantity at the lowest cost.

Efficiency may be defined as the relationship between goods or services produced and resources used to produce them. An efficient operation produces the maximum output for any given set of resource inputs; or, it has minimum inputs for any given quantity and quality of service provided.

Effectiveness may be defined as how well a programme or activity is achieving its established goals or other intended effects).

36. The Commission publishes reports of national studies which promote good management practice for specific services and functions. The auditor should apply the results of these studies at the audit unless there are specific and cogent reasons for not doing so. The auditor should consider carrying out local projects either in addition to or where appropriate instead of national studies. The choice of subject will have regard to the potential for improvement and significance to the authority. For both national and local projects the auditor must develop an effective system of monitoring the authority's progress in obtaining benefits identified at the current and earlier audits, and for encouraging action where required.

37. The achievement of economy, efficiency and effectiveness depends upon the existence of sound arrangements for the planning, appraisal, authorisation and control of the use of resources. It is management's responsibility to establish these arrangements and to ensure that they are working properly. The auditor's responsibility is to verify independently that these arrangements are in place and are effective.

38. The auditor will pay particular attention to good management practice, in, for example:

(a) Systems of planning, budgeting and controlling revenue and capital expenditure and income, and for allocating scarce resources.

(b) Manpower management, including arrangements for deciding and reviewing establishment levels and for recruiting, training, rewarding and otherwise motivating employees.

(c) Arrangements concerned with the proper management of all the assets of the authority - land, property (including the adequacy of arrangements for acquisition, maintenance, development, and disposal of land and buildings), plant, finance and energy.

(d) Arrangements designed to take advantage of economies of scale or skill, particularly in procurement of goods and services.

(e) Specific initiatives that have been taken to improve economy, efficiency and effectiveness in the performance of the wide variety of duties which have to be carried out by the authority.

(f) Proper codification of responsibilities, authority and accountability.

(g) Monitoring results against predetermined performance objectives and standards, to ensure that outstanding performance is encouraged and unacceptable performance corrected.

39. It is not the auditor's function to question policy. There is, however, a responsibility, particularly in the audit of local authorities, to consider the effects of policy and to examine the arrangements by which policy decisions are reached. To this end, the auditor should consider, for example:

(a) Whether policy objectives have been determined, and policy decisions taken, with appropriate authority.

(b) To what extent policy objectives are set, and decisions based, on sufficient, relevant and reliable financial and other data, and with the critical underlying assumptions made explicit.

(c) Whether there are satisfactory arrangements for considering alternative options, including the identification, selection and evaluation of such options.

(d) Whether established policy aims and objectives have been clearly set out; whether subsequent decisions on the implementation of policy are consistent with the approved aims and objectives, and have been taken with proper authority at the appropriate level; and whether the resultant instructions to staff accord with the approved policy aims and decisions and are clearly understood by those concerned.

(e) Whether there is conflict or potential conflict between different policy aims or objectives, or between the means chosen to implement them.

(f) Whether the costs of alternative levels of service have been considered, and are reviewed as costs and circumstances change.

40. In the case of health authorities the overall policy is determined by the Secretary of State. It is not for the auditor to question the policy objectives determined. However the auditor should review the decisions taken at the local level for the implementation of policy, to ensure that these are consistent with approved aims and objectives, and have been taken with proper authority at the appropriate level. The auditor should also consider whether the resultant instructions to staff accord with the approved policy aims and are clearly understood by those concerned.

3. REPORTING THE AUDIT

Auditor's Certificate and Opinion

41. The Act requires that when the audit is concluded, the auditor shall enter on the statement of accounts:

(a) a certificate that the audit has been completed in accordance with the Act;

(b) an opinion on the statement of accounts.

For authorities not required to prepare a statement of accounts, the auditor's certificate and opinion on the accounts must be entered on the books of accounts. All references in this code to statements of accounts should be read in this context.

42. The auditor's certificate should identify the accounts for the financial year to which the certificate of audit completion relates. The certificate should refer expressly to the fact that the audit has been completed in accordance with Part III of the Act in the case of local authorities and, in the case of health authorities, in accordance with Part I of the National Health Service and Community Care Act 1990, which amended Part III of the Local Government Finance Act 1982.

43. The auditor's certificate and opinion should identify those to whom it is addressed, the statements to which it relates and the date on which it is given. The auditor should refer expressly to the following:

(a) Whether the audit has been completed in accordance with the Code of Audit Practice.

(b) Whether the statement of accounts presents fairly the financial position of the authority at 31 March and its income and expenditure for the year then ended.

44. Non-principal authorities are not required by regulation to prepare statements of accounts. Accordingly, accounting conventions which are relevant to statements of accounts prepared by principal authorities, such as disclosure in footnotes of accounting policies and compliance with Statements of Standard Accounting Practice are inappropriate. In these circumstances, the audit opinion adopted for the audit of principal authorities may be varied where this is considered more appropriate. An example of a form of certificate and opinion is set out in the appendix.

45. As a general principle the auditor issuing an unqualified opinion should not make reference to specific aspects of the statement in the body of the opinion as such reference may be construed as being a qualification. In certain circumstances, however, readers will obtain a better understanding of the statement if their attention is drawn to important matters. Examples might include an unusual event, accounting policy or condition, awareness of which is fundamental to an understanding of the statement.

46. In order to avoid giving the impression that a qualification is intended, references which are meant as 'emphasis of matter' should appear after the opinion paragraph. Emphasis of matter should not be used to rectify a lack of appropriate disclosure in the statement of accounts, nor as a substitute for qualification.

47. The auditor's opinion is restricted to the statement of accounts which must be clearly identified. If, however, during the audit the auditor becomes aware of any matters affecting the validity of the supplementary information, eg, in local authorities, the explanatory foreword to the statement of accounts as required by the *Code of Practice on Local Authority Accounting*, consideration will need to be given to what action should be taken which according to the circumstances might be by referring to the matter in a report in the public interest or by covering it in the management letter.

48. When the auditor has concluded the audit, the Act requires a certificate to be entered on the statement of accounts that the audit has been completed as well as an opinion on the statement. Where the auditor has issued a report in the public interest in the course of or at the conclusion of the audit, this fact should be referred to in the certificate and opinion.

49. There will be occasions when the audit work is substantially completed but the audit cannot be closed, eg where, at local authority audits, because there are outstanding matters to be resolved arising from action or possible action under sections 17, 19 and 20 of the Act. Because proceedings under these sections may be time-consuming, the

auditor should consider issuing an opinion as soon as the necessary tests and procedures have been carried out subject to whatever qualification, if any, is considered appropriate.

50. Where an opinion is issued in advance of the conclusion of the audit, the auditor must consider the effect of significant events which occur between the date of any such opinion on the statement of accounts and the date on which, by section 18 of the Act, the certification of completion and opinion is entered on the statement of accounts.

Qualification to an Auditor's Opinion

51. The auditor should specify the nature of the circumstances giving rise to a qualification as to whether the statement of accounts presents fairly the financial position of the authority. In general, these will fall into one of two categories:

(a) Where there is an uncertainty which prevents the auditor from forming an opinion on a matter (uncertainty), or

(b) Where the auditor is able to form an opinion on a matter but this conflicts with the view given by the statement of accounts (disagreement).

52. A 'disclaimer of opinion' and an 'adverse opinion' are the extreme forms of the two main categories of qualification arising from uncertainty and disagreement. In most situations, a 'subject to' or 'except' form of opinion will be appropriate. The disclaimer of opinion or adverse opinion should be regarded as measures of last resort. Where the auditor has qualified the opinion on the statement of accounts attention should be drawn to this fact in a report in the public interest which should refer to any more detailed explanation which may be required.

53. An auditor should only qualify the audit opinion where the matter is material in the context of the statement of accounts. In general terms, a matter should be judged to be material if knowledge of the matter would be likely to influence the general impression of the authority's financial position formed by a user of the statement. Materiality should be considered in the context of the statement as a whole, the balance sheets, the revenue accounts, and individual items within the statement.

54. Where the auditor has decided that a matter is sufficiently material to warrant a qualification of the opinion, the auditor must then determine whether or not the matter is so fundamental as to require either an adverse opinion or a disclaimer of opinion on the statement of accounts as a whole. An uncertainty becomes fundamental when its potential impact on the statement could be so great as to render it as a whole misleading. A disagreement becomes fundamental when its impact on the statement is so great as to render it totally misleading. The combined effect of all uncertainties and disagreements must be considered.

55. All reasons for the qualification should be given together with a quantification of its effect on the statement of accounts if this is both relevant and practicable. Sufficient detail should be included so as to leave the reader in no doubt as to its meaning and its implications for an understanding of the statement. A copy of any qualified opinion should be sent to the Commission, and in the case of a health authority also to the Secretary of State.

56. The forms of certificate and opinion which auditors should adopt and examples are set out in the appendix.

Report in the Public Interest

57. The Act requires that the auditor shall consider whether, in the public interest, a report should be made on any matter which comes to the auditor's attention in the course of the audit in order that it may be considered by the body concerned or brought to the attention of the public. The auditor shall also consider whether the public interest requires any such matter to be made the subject of an immediate report rather than of a report to be made at the conclusion of the audit. If the report is an immediate report, a copy is to be sent to the Commission, and, in the case of a health authority to the Secretary of State, forthwith. Otherwise a copy of any report is to be sent not later than fourteen days after the conclusion of the audit. Copies of reports issued to district health authorities or family health service authorities should be sent also to the appropriate regional health authority, or in Wales to the Health Finance Management Division of the Welsh Office.

58. It is for the auditor to decide when to make a report in the public interest. Examples of the kinds of matters which, if significant, would call for a report are as follows:

(a)   The fact that the auditor's opinion on the statement of accounts has been qualified, and conclusions therefrom.

(b)   Delayed preparation of accounts.

(c)   Failure to comply with statutory requirements.

(d)   Excessive or inadequate levels of balances, inappropriate levels of provisions, lack of prudence, prospective budget deficits, and other similar financial matters calling for comment.

(e)   Lack of action on matters previously reported by the auditor, including previously identified value for money opportunities.

(f)   Absence of or weaknesses in arrangements for securing economy, efficiency and effectiveness in the use of resources.

(g)   Unnecessary expenditure or loss of income due to waste, extravagance, inefficient financial administration, poor value for money, mistake or other cause.

(h)   Weaknesses in management information systems and monitoring arrangements.

(i)   High levels of arrears, deficiencies in income collection procedures.

(j)   Deficiencies in internal control arrangements (including internal audit).

(k)   Objections received at the audit of local authorities and action under section 19, 20, 25A and 25D of the Act.

(l)   Misconduct, frauds, or special investigations.

59. In general a report should only be made where the auditor considers a matter sufficiently important to be brought to the notice of the authority or the public. The test of 'materiality', however, which applies to the auditor's opinion on the statement of accounts (see paragraph 53) is not relevant when the auditor is deciding whether to issue a report in the public interest.

60. The auditor should not be deflected from making a report because its subject matter is critical or unwelcome, if it is considered in the public interest to do so. The auditor is able to form an independent and impartial view on how an authority is conducting its affairs and these reports are an important means of informing the public. Auditors should bear these considerations in mind when deciding whether or not to make a report. It is not, however, the function of the auditor to express an opinion as to the wisdom of particular decisions taken by authorities in the lawful exercise of their discretion. Any report relating to such decisions should only refer to any facts which have not previously

been brought to the notice of the authority or which ought to be brought to the attention of the public.

61. Although criticism of past performance may sometimes be necessary when reporting, the auditor should aim to be constructive and avoid language which generates defensiveness and opposition. The emphasis in the report should be on the steps necessary to effect improvement.

62. The auditor should arrange meetings with members and officers in order to discuss with them matters which it is intended to include in the report. Such meetings afford an opportunity to go into matters in greater detail than may be practicable in a report and allow individuals to answer any criticism that the auditor proposes to make. The auditor will then be in a position to take account of these discussions and where appropriate to indicate what action has been agreed.

63. Where appropriate, matters which may give rise to a report should be conveyed to those responsible in writing during the progress of an audit so that early corrective action can be taken. This does not relieve the auditor of the duty to consider whether in due course a report in the public interest should be submitted.

Management letters

64. The management letter should summarise those matters of significance which the auditor has raised during the audit. It will also summarise the benefits anticipated from implementation of agreed actions. The draft management letter should be discussed with the officers concerned. It will then provide the agenda for a meeting which the auditor should seek with appropriate members to explain and amplify the nature of any concerns and to respond to members' questions. In its final form the management letter should be addressed and submitted to all the members of the authority in question. Where the authority does not arrange for distribution to all members, the auditor should do so. A copy of the management letter should be sent to the Commission. Management letters for regional health authorities, special health authorities and NHS trusts should be copied to the Secretary of State. Those for district health authorities and family health service authorities in England should be copied to the appropriate regional health authority and those in Wales to the Secretary of State.

65. The auditor should submit a management letter as soon as is practicable, and, except where there are exceptional circumstances, by the 31 December following the end of the financial year to which the accounts relate.

4. AUDIT OF LOCAL AUTHORITIES

66. In addition to the general duties of auditors referred to in Parts 1, 2 and 3, above, the auditor of a local authority has particular responsibilities to the public and exercises special powers under the Act which are set out below.

Responsibilities to the public

67. The auditor must at all times keep in mind the responsibilities to members of the public. The Act gives members of the public wide powers to inspect accounts, question the auditor and make objections to the accounts.

68. The auditor should take note of information received from the public. Apart from the statutory rights of local government electors to question the auditor and to make

objections at audit, any person may at any time give information to the auditor which concerns the accounts of a body under audit or is otherwise relevant to the auditor's functions. Where appropriate, the auditor should remind an elector of the right to make an objection to the accounts.

69. Where any representations are made or information is given relevant to the audit, the auditor should consider whether the matter is such as to merit prompt investigation. If a local government elector wishes to make an objection and the matter appears to be of such urgency that it needs to be heard before any date appointed for the making of objections pursuant to regulations of the Act, the auditor should consider drawing the attention of the elector to the rights under section 22(1)(a) to apply to the Commission for an extraordinary audit. The auditor should also consider whether to make a report to the Commission so that it may consider whether an extraordinary audit is desirable.

Exercise of Section 19 and 20 powers

70. The auditor has special powers under section 19 of the Act (application to the court for a declaration that an item of account is unlawful) and section 20 (recovery of amounts not accounted for, etc). These powers must be exercised personally and ensure that all persons who may be affected by their exercise have a fair and adequate opportunity to reply to any allegations or charges which are critical of or adverse to them.

Questions and Objections

71. The auditor should not admit questions on general matters such as the authority's policies, finances or procedures which are not about the actual accounts for the year to which the date referred to in paragraph 69 relates. Nor without the consent of the authority should the auditor disclose any information about transactions reflected in the accounts which is not disclosed in the accounts, books, deeds, contracts, bills, vouchers and receipts required to be made available under the Regulations. The auditor should not disclose personal information about the remuneration or other benefits paid to a .member of the authority's staff.

72. On receipt of a notice of objection, the auditor should ensure that a copy has been supplied to the authority and should verify that the proposed objection relates to the relevant year of account and that it relates to a matter to which the auditor's powers are applicable and is otherwise valid in law as an objection within the meaning of the Act.

73. Notice of the objection should be given to any persons who may be affected by a decision upon the objection in order that they may have an opportunity to deal with any matter adverse to them.

74. Before determination of the objection, the auditor should make whatever enquiries are considered necessary into the subject- matter of the objection. Any documents or information which are material to a decision on the objection should be made available to the objector and to other parties.

75. There is no statutory requirement that an oral hearing of all parties must be held to determine an objection. The auditor must consider whether justice or the public interest would be best served by giving those affected the opportunity of an oral hearing and, if so, whether that hearing should be in public. Where there is an oral hearing all persons concerned should be given due notice to be present or represented at the hearing to deal with any matters affecting them.

76. At such a hearing the onus is on the objector to submit evidence to prove any allegation made. The body under audit and any individuals concerned must be given the

opportunity of answering the objection and submitting evidence. The auditor should afford opportunity for the cross-examination of witnesses. If it becomes apparent that injustices may be caused by allegations made without due notice, the public should be excluded.

77. The auditor's decision should be communicated to any persons who may be affected by it. The auditor should inform an objector of the rights of appeal against an adverse decision and the procedures relating thereto. Any statement of reasons, normally to be sent to the objector by recorded delivery, should indicate with precision the grounds on which a decision is based. It should deal with all the substantial points which have been raised and be sufficiently full and clear to enable the person aggrieved, and the court in the event of an appeal, to see what matters the auditor has taken into consideration and what view has been reached on the points of fact and law which arise.

Exercise of powers under Sections 25A and 25D

78. The auditor has special powers under section 25A of the Act (power to issue a prohibition order) and section 25D of the Act (power to apply for judicial review). These powers supplement and are additional to other powers available to auditors. These powers should be used only where the matter is significant either in amount or principle or both.

79. There is no duty on the auditor to seek out matters which might be the subject of the issue of a prohibition order or an application for judicial review. The auditor should give consideration to matters which arise in the course of normal audit duties and matters raised by members and officers of the body under the audit and by members of the public. However, local government electors have no rights of question or objection in relation to these powers corresponding to those conferred by section 17 of the 1982 Act. The auditor should give particular consideration to any report made by a chief finance officer or a monitoring officer drawing attention to possible unlawful expenditure, course of action leading to loss or deficiency or entry of an item of account, or a likelihood of expenditure exceeding resources.

80. So far as is consistent with the prompt exercise of the powers in the public interest, auditors should give the body under audit or officer concerned an opportunity to respond to the matters giving cause for concern, albeit that it may only be possible to give the body or officer a very short period to respond. However, there is no statutory requirement on the auditor to consult with the body under audit before the issue of a prohibition order or seeking leave to commence proceedings for judicial review. In some circumstances, it may not be appropriate to give notice to the body under audit or relevant officer prior to taking action.

5. AUDIT OF HEALTH SERVICE BODIES

81. In addition to the duties of auditors referred to in Parts 1, 2 and 3, above, the auditor of a health authority has particular responsibilities which are set out below.

82. The auditor has special duties under section 20(3) of the National Health Service and Community Care Act 1990 to report forthwith to the Secretary of State where it is believed that an authority's or officer's decision would involve unlawful expenditure or that the authority's or officer's action would be unlawful and cause a loss or deficiency.

83. There is no duty on the auditor to seek out matters for referral to the Secretary of State. The auditor should give consideration to matters arising in the course of normal audit duties and matters raised by members and officers of the body under audit and by

others. The auditor should give particular consideration to any report made by any officer of the authority drawing attention to possible unlawful expenditure, course of action leading to loss or deficiency or entry of an item of account, or a likelihood of expenditure exceeding resources.

84. So far as is consistent with the prompt exercise of the powers, auditors should give the body under audit or officer concerned an opportunity to respond to the matters giving cause for concern, albeit that it may only be possible to give the body or officer a very short period to respond. However, there is no statutory requirement on the auditor to consult with the body or officer under audit before referring a matter to the Secretary of State. In some circumstances, it may not be appropriate to give notice to the body under audit or relevant officer prior to taking action.

General Practice Fund Holders

85. When examining the accounts of general practice fund holders, which are summarised to form part of the accounts of family health services authorities, the auditor should seek to rely on analytical review techniques with any detailed audit procedures carried out on a cyclical basis.

Appendix

EXAMPLES OF THE FORMS OF OPINION AND CERTIFICATE ON STATEMENTS OF ACCOUNTS

Unqualified Audit Opinion

(Name of authority)

I/We certify that I/we have completed the audit of the authority's accounts for the year ended 31 March, 19.. in accordance with Part III of the Local Government Finance Act 1982/Part I of the National Health Service and Community Care Act 1990* and the Code of Audit Practice.

In my/our opinion the statement of accounts set out on pages ... to ... presents fairly the financial position of the authority at 31 March, 19.. and its income and expenditure for the year then ended.

Auditor

(Date)

* Reference should be made to the Local Government Finance Act 1982 when certifying the completion of local authority audits, with reference made to the National Health Service and Community Care Act 1990 when certifying the completion of health authority audits.

Unqualified Audit Opinion issued in advance of the conclusion of audit

(Name of authority)

The audit of the authority's accounts for the year ended 31 March, 19.. has been carried out in accordance with Part III of the Local Government Finance Act 1982/Part I of the National Health Service and Community Care Act 1990 and the Code of Audit Practice and has been substantially completed.

** The audit cannot be formally concluded, however, because ....

I/we am/are satisfied that the amounts involved in the subject matters concerned cannot have a material effect on the statement of accounts.

In my/our opinion the statement of accounts set out on pages ... to ... presents fairly the financial position of the authority at 31 March, 19.. and its income and expenditure for the year then ended.

Auditor

(Date)

** The auditor will need to consider whether the inclusion of such a paragraph adds to the reader's understanding of the opinion.

Unqualified Audit Opinion where the auditor has issued a report in the public interest in the course of the audit

(Name of authority)

I/We certify that I/we have completed the audit of the authority's accounts for the year ended 31 March, 19.. in accordance with Part III of the Local Government Finance Act 1982/Part I of the National Health Service and Community Care Act 1990 and the Code of Audit Practice.

A report in the public interest referring to delays in preparing the authority's accounts for the financial year ended 31 March, 19.. was submitted to the authority on .... 19..

In my/our opinion the statement of accounts set out on pages ... to ... presents fairly the financial position of the authority at 31 March, 19.. and its income and expenditure for the year then ended.

Auditor

(Date)

Unqualified Audit Opinion - Example of emphasis of matters

(Name of authority)

I/We certify that I/we have completed the audit of the authority's accounts for the year ended 31 March, 19.. in accordance with Part III of the Local Government Finance Act 1982/Part I of the National Health Service and Community Care Act 1990 and the Code of Audit Practice.

In my/our opinion the statement of accounts set out on pages ... to ... presents fairly the financial position of the authority at 31 March, 19.. and its income and expenditure for the year then ended.

Without qualifying our opinion above I/we draw attention to note ... which refers to a change in accounting policy whereby interest on loans which was previously accounted for on a cash payments basis has been accrued up to 31 March, 19... The additional charge to revenue resulting from this change amounted to £....

Auditor

(Date)

Qualified Audit Opinions

Example 1

Uncertainty - Material but not fundamental
'Subject to' opinion - estimate of grant due

(Name of local authority)

I/We certify that I/we have completed the audit of the authority's accounts for the year ended 31 March, 19.. in accordance with Part III of the Local Government Finance Act 1982 and the Code of Audit Practice.

Government grant claims for housing benefit subsidy have not been finalised by the Council since 19... Discussions are currently taking place with the Department of Social Security to clarify difficulties over their completion. The statement of accounts consequently includes an amount of £... based on the best estimate of grant due to the Council.

Subject to the effects of any adjustments that might be shown to be necessary on the finalisation of the housing benefit subsidy claims, in my/our opinion the statement of accounts on pages ... to ... presents fairly the financial position of the authority at 31 March, 19... and its income and expenditure for the year then ended.

Auditor

(Date)

(Name of health authority)

I/We certify that I/we have completed the audit of the authority's accounts for the year ended 31 March, 19... in accordance with Part I of the National Health Service and Community Care Act 1990 and the Code of Audit Practice.

It has not been possible to verify the figures shown for stock in the accounts due to a failure of the stock ledger system. The statement of accounts consequently includes an amount of £... based on management's estimate of normal stock levels.

Subject to the effects of any adjustments that might have been necessary if adequate stock records had been available, in my/our opinion the statement of accounts on pages ... to ... presents fairly the financial position of the authority at 31 March 19... and its income and expenditure for the year then ended.

Auditor

(Date)

Example 2

Disagreement - Material but not fundamental
'Except' opinion - Inadequate provision for doubtful debts

(Name of authority)

I/We certify that I/we have completed the audit of the authority's accounts for the year ended 31 March, 19.. in accordance with Part III of the Local Government Finance Act 1982/Part I of the National Health Service and Community Care Act 1990 and the Code of Audit Practice.

Of the £... shown as being owed to the authority at the 31 March, 19... £... relates to services supplied over xx years ago. In my/our opinion it is likely that a substantial portion of the debts will not be recoverable; the amount not recoverable cannot reasonably be estimated at this time but is likely to exceed the existing provision for doubtful debts of £... by a substantial amount.

Except that the provision for doubtful debts does not appear adequate, in my/our opinion the statement of accounts set out on pages ... to ... presents fairly the financial position of the authority at 31 March 19... and its income and expenditure for the year then ended.

Auditor

(Date)

Form of Certificate to be given on conclusion of the audit where an earlier opinion has been issued

(Name of authority)

I/We certify that I/we have completed the audit of the authority's accounts for the year ended 31 March, 19.. in accordance with Part III of the Local Government Finance Act 1982/Part I of the National Health Service and Community Care Act 1990 and the Code of Audit Practice.

As stated in my/our opinion issued on ... the statement of accounts set out on pages ... to ... in my/our opinion presents fairly the financial position of the authority at 31 March, 19.. and its income and expenditure for the year then ended

or

As stated in my/our opinion issued on ... the statement of accounts set out on pages ... to ... in my/our opinion presents fairly the financial position of the authority at 31 March, 19... and its income and expenditure for the year then ended subject to/except for the reason(s) given in my/our opinion.

Auditor

(Date)

Unqualified Audit Opinion at Non-principal Authorities

(Name of authority)

I/We certify that I/we have completed the audit of the authority's accounts for the year ended 31 March, 19.. in accordance with Part III of the Local Government Finance Act 1982/Part I of the National Health Service and Community Care Act 1990 and the Code of Audit Practice.

In my/our opinion the accounts record fairly the financial transactions of the authority, for the year then ended.

Auditor

(Date)

APPENDIX D

UNREPORTED AUDIT CASES

D.6,n.2 The cited provision was repealed by the Local Government and Housing Act 1989, which introduced a new regime for capital finance of local authorities.

D.11 The decision in *Wilkinson* v. *Doncaster M.B.C,* was upheld by the Court of Appeal (1985), 84 L.G.R. 257.

D.12 The case here summarised has been reported *sub nom Commission for Local Authority Accounts in Scotland* v. *Stirling D.C.,* 1984 S.L.T. 442.

APPENDIX E

PRECEDENTS

E.2 Is no longer applicable to immediate reports on local government audits, see 4.105, 4.110A, above, E.2A, below.

E.2A Notice of rights of inspection of auditor's immediate report.

See 4.110A, above

(NAME OF BODY)

AUDIT OF ACCOUNTS

INSPECTION OF AUDITOR'S REPORT

Local Government Finance Act 1982, s.18A

NOTICE is given that:

(1) the auditor of the accounts of the above – named body for the year ended 31 March 19   has made a report on [a];

(2) the report is available for inspection by any member of the public at (place) on working days between the hours of (time) and (time) [b], when any such person may make copies of the report or extracts therefrom;

(3) copies of the report will be delivered to any such person on payment of (reasonable sum in light of copying costs) for each copy of the report.

Dated this   day of   19

(Name and office)

Notes

[a] Insert words identifying the subject-matter of the report.

[b] Parochial and other small authorities might insert any reasonable restriction which may be necessary as to the days on which the report is available, and, if appropriate, add 'or by arrangement'.

E.3 Because of the amendments to section 16 of the 1982 Act referred to at 4.112, above, it may be desirable to insert the words 'my functions under the above Act in' between 'of' and 'auditing' in the first line of the suggested Requirement.

E.3,n.1 For 's.437(1), Companies Act 1948', read 's.725, Companies Act 1985'.

E.7 The note on page 379 is no longer applicable: 9.2-4, 9.6, above.

E.7,n.2 For '1985' edition of *Supreme Court Practice*, read '1991'.

INDEX

Internal drainage boards
National Rivers Authority acting as 2 3
Item of account contrary to law 6.1-40E,
  see also Illegality; Order for repayment;
  Special jurisdiction of auditor; Unlawful
  exercise of discretion; *Ultra vires*
  declaration by court 6.158
  incidental powers 6.22A-G
  miscellaneous items 1.54I, 6.32A
  rectification of accounts 6.194
  value for money work, relationship 4.77A
Joint authorities
  audit 2.3, 2.30A
  statements of accounts 3.41
Judicial aspects of auditor's duties 10.2-17
Judicial review
  application by auditor 5.41Q-X
    auditor's discretion 5.41U
    Code of Audit Practice 5.41X
    definition of auditor 5.41W
  auditor's decisions, of 1.54I, 9.36A-D
  authorities' decisions, of, generally
    8.49-52A
Loan redemption 3.16
Loans and capital finance 3.16-18
Loans funds 3.17
  advances in excess of borrowing powers
    3.17A, 6.32A
Loans, internal 3.18
Local government electors, representatives
  8.25A-B
Local government/health service auditors,
  see also Auditors; General duties etc.;
  Health service auditors; Special
  jurisdiction etc.
  admissions/confessions to 10.55-8
  comparison, company auditors 4.4-7
  documents etc., powers as to, *see* that title
  independence 2.79-80
  qualifications 2.66
London boroughs - application of *ultra vires*
  6.6
Loss, wilful misconduct, 7.42-64, *see also*
  Special jurisdiction of auditor
  assessment, sums certified due 7.67-72
  disqualification 7.62
  failure to raise income required by law
    1.54B-C, 7.58-61D
  loss through waste 7.50A
  sincerity of motive 7.42
  value for money work, relationship 4.77A
Management letters 4.111
Mandatory/directory requirements 6.9
Members, delegation to 6.116-8
Misconduct, *see* Loss, wilful misconduct
Monitoring officers 6.40D
Motive, sincerity of 7.42

National Health Service, *see* Health service
  accounts, Health service auditors,
  Health service bodies
National Rivers Authority 2.3
Natural justice 10.18-47
  audit proceedings, application to 10.21A,
    10.25, 10.33, 10.36-37B, 10.45
  bias, rule against 10.19-21A
  fair hearing 10.25-44
  hearings, oral, by auditor, *see* that title
  opposing case, right to know 10.34A
  ss.19, 20 L.G.F. Act 1982, application
    to 10.45-7
Nature of auditor's duties – judicial or otherwise 10.2-17
NHS Trusts
  accounts 3.24A
  audit provisions 2.30E,G
Notice of audit hearings 10.67
Notice of public rights – parochial
  authorities 4.105, 8.6
Oath, evidence on 4.130-1
Objections at audit 8.36-43
  admission of public 10.80-3
  appeals from auditors, *see* that title
  attendance at audit 8.43, 10.37A-B
  evidence, *see* that title
  hearing by audit staff 2.71
  judicial review and 8.52A
  natural justice, *see* that title
  representative, by 8.25A-B
Offences
  audit reports, inspection/copies 4.110
Officers
  chief finance officer 6.40A-C
  delegation to 6.115-8
  health service, audit of accounts of 2.31
  illegality, reports on 6.40A-E
  monitoring officer 6.40D
  responsible financial officer 3.29, 6.40A-C
Opinion on accounts, auditor's 4.63-5
Oral hearings, *see* Hearings, oral, by auditor
Order for repayment, illegal expenditure
  6.163-87
  authorising, responsibility 6.163
  bankruptcy of person responsible 6.183-7
  enforcement 6.183-8
Parish meetings 2.11
Parochial authorities – notice of public
  rights 4.105, 8.6
Passenger transport 2.18-24
  subsidiary companies 2.20-24
Police authorities 2.14-15
Policy/administration
  auditors' reports 4.90-93A
Precedents
  requirement, access to documents App.E.3